PLANNING FOR ACADEMIC EXCELLENCE

ABOUT THE AUTHOR

DR. S.S. GUPTA (born 1-1-1929) currently Vice-Chancellor of the Agra University, is a D. Litt. in Economics. He worked as a Principal for 13 years and made bold experiments. He tried to give new direction to N.S.S., N.C.C, Proctorial Ministry of the College, College Library, College Buildings, Keeping of College Accounts, etc. He tried to place a Principal-Teacher, Principal-Non-Teacher and Principal-Students relationships on new foundations. He tried to develop in all a sense of belonging to and pride in the institution. It all gave excellent results and the college was given U.P. Merit Award twice. During his tenure of 13 years as Principal, almost 50 teachers earned Ph.D. degrees and almost 250 students were registered for their Ph.D. degrees in the Faculties of Arts, Science, Education and Law. But his tenure abruptly ended in discomfiture. The College Management could not relish his popularity. It encouraged teacher-politics and patted rowdy students. Principal Gupta was physically assaulted twice for not permitting copying in the examinations or allowing misappropriation or embezzlement of funds. Ultimately Dr. Gupta preferred to take pre-mature retirement, two years earlier than the due time of superannuation.

Dr. Gupta has written several thought provoking books. Most of his research articles and Survey Reports have been published.

PLANNING
FOR
ACADEMIC EXCELLENCE

SHANTI SWARUP GUPTA
Vice-Chancellor
Agra University, Agra

CONCEPT PUBLISHING COMPANY, NEW DELHI-110059

ISBN 81-7022-444-6

First Published 1992

Published and Printed by
Ashok Kumar Mittal
Concept Publishing Company
A/15-16, Commercial Block, Mohan Garden
NEW DELHI-110059 (India)

Lasertypeset by
Microtech Advance Printing Systems (Pvt.) Ltd.
H-13, Bali Nagar
NEW DELHI-110015

To

My Daughter-in-Law

Viniti

FOREWORD

As of 1988-89, 83.4 per cent of the total number of students in the higher educational system were studying in 6,912 colleges affiliated to various universities. Many of these colleges are non-viable, poorly managed, inadequately funded and incompetently administered. Regretfully, the colleges have been neglected by all concerned since 1950s, though it is too patent that no change in the higher educational scene in the country is possible unless there is all-around improvement in the colleges.

The Principal acts as the king-pin in college administration and on his equipment, capabilities and vision depend the achievement and image of the institution. A balanced and imaginative comprehension of the physical set-up of the college – the quality, quantity and location of the infrastructure facilities i.e., its buildings, hostels, play-ground, laboratories, libraries, student facilities etc., the man-power requirements and their equipment and training including that of the teachers and administrative and library staff, management of college finances and tapping the funding agencies, inter-action with the community around and extra-curricular activities, conduct of examinations, perspective planning for development of the college and admissions policy, and above all ensuring excellence in teaching and research, and similar other basic ingredients which contribute to the over-all excellence of a college, have to form part of the necessary equipment of a principal. No analytical study on the role of a college Principal had yet been brought out by any mature educational administrator-cum-scholar.

Dr. S.S. Gupta, Vice Chancellor, Agra University, who has earlier worked as a Principal of a reputed college in Aligarh, for a long period of thirteen years, has done yeoman service in bringing out this excellent publication: *Planning for Academic Excellence*. This book will not only help a teacher who is going to step-in as a principal of a college, but serve as a permanent guide and manual for all those who are involved in college management in any capacity. Dr. Gupta has looked at the subject essentially from the view-point as to what the equipment and potentialities of a good principal ought to be – what should he aim at, how should he go about performing his duties and responsibilities, what hurdles is he likely to encounter in each area of college administration and how to overcome them. The book presents a comprehensive and unified picture, with uncanny details of each component of college administration. The various funding agencies at the Centre and the U.G.C. sponsored schemes for colleges have also been discussed. The Principal's role has been delineated in a wider frame of reference of the main thrusts of the National Policy on Education, 1986 and the Programme of Action. Dr. Gupta deserves the gratitude of all those concerned with educational administration, for bringing out this extremely utilitarian book.

It may appear after reading the book that hardly could a person be endowed with all the qualities and equipment expected of him to perform a Principal's job. This, in a sense, is true. One equips himself either through training, or through trial and error while on the job. This prominently brings out the need for a thorough training of the Principals who have freshly embarked upon their responsibilities, as also of those who require exposure to certain inputs as regards college administration. The State Government, NIEPA and other organisations associated with training could gainfully take note of this necessity.

The book was, perhaps, conceived a couple of years back in 1987 when a workshop for principals was organized and conducted by Dr. Gupta, in Agra University, to discuss the problems faced by them in college administration. I happened to be the Vice Chancellor, then, I, therefore, feel extremely happy that the exercise undertaken then has culminated in such a rewarding publication.

I do hope and wish that this study would induce scholars to bring out several other publications on the problems related to collegiate education.

I am glad to commend this book to the readers.

PROF. S.K. AGRAWALA

Secretary, Association of Indian Universities,
and
former Vice-Chancellor, Agra University

AIU House, 16 Kotla Marg
New Delhi 110002
February 2, 1992

PREFACE

It was on June 20, 1974 that all of a sudden I was asked to take over the Principalship of a very big Post-graduate College at Aligarh, where I had already served for twenty-four years in various capacities. Soon after, I realised that my handicaps to discharge the arduous task of a Principal were many. I have no idea of the financial control and management. How to plan a library had never struck me. What are the requisites of a laboratory was beyond my comprehension. What are the essentials of a college buildings? The list appeared to be endless. I looked helplessly and sought for advice. I soon realised that other Principals were no better placed. Then I tried to equip myself the hard way.

I talked about this deficiency of Principals to my Vice-Chancellor, Dr. S.N. Mehrotra who is a knowledgeable person. He managed to send two of us to NIEPA, Delhi. NIEPA was organising Principal's workshop. They selected about thirty Principals from all over the country and gave them exposure to the latest trends in education for three weeks. It was a good exposure but failed to help the Principals in solving their problems. What is the goal of Indian education? What is the meaning of an elite college and how to solve day-to-day problems did not fall under their syllabus.

I talked, after a few years, to my new Vice-Chancellor, Dr. S.K. Agrawala, who was a well meaning person, about organising a Principal's Workshop, where common problems may be discussed and experiences exchanged. I was asked to organise it and the University Grants Commission, New Delhi funded it. It proved to be the first effort in the right direction.

After retirement I thought of writing a book which would be helpful to a new Principal in knowing basics and thinking and acting on right lines. I thought even two steps in the right direction might be beneficial for all.

I know this book is not a comprehensive one; but I think it will provoke better qualified persons to guide the future Principals in a more meaningful way. At the same time it will help Principals in making bold experiments on the right lines and enrich one another with new experiences. I trust and believe that the net result will be an onward march towards a quality-oriented education.

In writing this book several friends have helped me in innumerable ways. I am specially indebted to Prof. N.L. Sharma, Prof. B.B. Mittal, Prof. V.P. Mittal, Shri Surendra Agarwal, Shri B.K. Sharma, Km. Vindu Gupta, Dr. Mahesh Prasad, Dr. M.P. Awasthi, Dr. K.N. Gaur and Smt. Archana Agarwal. Thanks to them all.

S.S. GUPTA

CONTENTS

LIST OF FIGURES AND TABLES

FIGURES

TABLES

1

WHAT SHOULD I TRY TO ACHIEVE?

On becoming a principal, the first question that one ought to address to one-self is: What should I try to achieve in my tenure as a Principal?

Know Thy Self

Before trying to answer this question, a knowledge and realistic assessment of the following essentials is necessary :

1. *The students :* An educational institution is started to educate students. Its fame depends upon the quality of the students it produces. And the quality of end-products has certainly a relationship with the quality of students admitted. In a limited period – when a student enters the college and leaves it — some thing spectacular cannot be achieved, so the Principal should have a very clear idea about the students seeking admission in the institution. Are they coming from villages or cities? Do they belong to the first generation of learners? What is their financial status? What is their cultural background? What are their academic achievements? It is often seen that children of farmers are neither very good at studies nor much disciplined, nor have high aspirations. The sons and daughters of neo-rich class are not serious about studies and take pleasure in organising groups and creating problems. So, a Principal, who has a keen desire to do something, must know about the academic achievements, aspirations, habits, financial position, etc., of the students seeking admission in the college.
2. *The Teachers* — Today teaching is a profession like any other professions. Most of the teachers are not teachers because of any idealism. They are there because they could not get any-

thing, better. Yet these teachers are the main architect of student's life. So the Principal must have a clear assessment about them. What are their academic achievement? How much sincere are they towards their job? How much disciplined are they? What are their good points and what are their bad points? How much change can be brought about in them through persuation or admonition?

3. *The non-teachers* — Class three and class four employees are an equally important component of an educational institution as are teachers and students. With a disciplined and efficient office, much better results can be obtained and with an inefficient, corrupt and indisciplined staff, probably nothing can be achieved. So, a Principal should have a very clear idea about the competency, honesty, sincerity and loyalty of the non-teaching staff members.
4. *The Secretary and Members of the Management* — Today most of the colleges are private colleges managed by a Secretary and a Board of Management. Those days are gone when very respectable people of the town, who had no axe to grind, used to be elected as Secretary and members of the Board of Management. They used to grace the chair and paid due respect to the Principal and teachers and, as a rule, interferred the least in the day-to-day administration of the college. Today elections for the membership of Board of Management are contested on party lines and all tactics are used to come into power. Today, social recognition is acquired, through the membership of the college Managing Committees by otherwise non-entities. They do not understand the intricacies of the college management and are keen on showing themselves off. Quite an appreciable number of them want to make money also. No college can function smoothly without a very good rapport between the Principal and the Board of Management, specially the Secretary. So, the college Principal must have a very clear understanding of what type of people are at the helm of affairs and to what extent can he take them with him.
5. *The Vice-Chancellor and the University* — Today, Vice-Chancellors, by and large, are not pure academicians. Most of them manage to get the post through political manipulations or, as is now increasingly said, through other means. So, such

persons, in turn have different norms of behaviour and working. The Principal should have very clear concept of the key persons manning the University, the working of the university and the important Acts, Statutes, Ordinances, Rules, etc., of the University.

6. *The Directorate and the Ministry of Education* — Except in U.P., the role of the Directorate and the Ministry of Education of a state is not much in evidence in directly shaping the destiny of a college. Yet the Principal should have a close knowledge of the working of these two important wings of the government because, at times of need, he may know whom to approach, how to approach and what to do.
7. *The District Administration* — Today no academic institution can think of functioning smoothly, not to say efficiently, if the Principal has not the knowledge of and acquaintance with the important officers of the District such as District Magistrate, Suptd. of Police, District Inspector of Schools, Treasury officer, etc., and an insight of the functioning of these government departments.

The Direction

The Principal, who wants to achieve something, should, after the assessment of the above seven essentials pose another question to himself, namely what are the aims or what should be the aims of the Indian Education? A knowledge of these aims will set direction in which a Principal has to work and march *vis-a-vis* his institution.

It is unfortunate that even after forty years of independence, no official document has tried to spell out the aims of the Indian Education. India is a very old country with a very definite and distinct culture, value-system and aspirations. The aims of the Indian Education should reflect all this. To my mind, the aim of the Indian Education should be to develop in a student those qualities which may give him, at the end of the last ladder of formal education, a balanced, developed and integrated personality. In other words, end-products must have:

A. *Physical Development*

Man's body is the most important thing in life. The proverb is 'a sound body has a sound mind'. Further, without a sound body one will neither be able to enjoy one's material possessions nor enjoy life, nor be even able to do good to others. Hence, the primary aim of education should be to help students in the development of their physique. The aim should be to make the body free from ailments, improve stamina as per individual's constitution and make it capable to withstand the strains of todays life.

To be physically fit, a student must be made aware of the importance of regular physical exercises; cleanliness of the body, living place and environment; regularity and punctuality in life; balanced dietary habits, etc.

B. *Intellectual Development*

Education should make man not only literate, having knowledge of as many subjects as possible or specialised knowledge of one or two subjects but also develop in him a scientific outlook, a capacity to differentiate between right and wrong and take rational decisions in real life. It must give him practical orientation.

C. *Moral Development*

Man is a social being. To run society on healthy lines man must follow those norms of behaviour which were developed by our ancestors. Education should develop in a student such moral values as truth, simplicity, love, self-control, non-anger, non-stealing, reasonable attachment with material things, emphasis on spiritualism, etc. It must tell the meaning of these moral values and give him practical lessons how to imbibe them.

D. *Patriotism and Universalism*

At present, two divergent tendencies are clearly visible in the world. When some natural calamity befall any part of a country, the whole world rushes to its rescue. Food-stuffs, money and medicines and other relief material start pouring in from all over the world. A laudable phase indeed. However, either in the name of national interest or ideology, the world is getting divided into blocks and one block is trying to exploit the other. This is not a happy trend, this must be checked.

Just as education, through moral lessons, teaches subjugation of self interest to the social and national interests, similarly, it should also teach love for the world through patriotism. In patriotism, one makes sacrifices for the nation. Once this tendency takes roots then the next step can easily follow. Patriotism can certainly help in developing, a sense of universal brotherhood without sacrificing reasonable national interests.

E. *Spiritual Development*

Modern scientists have grudgingly started accepting the existence of some super natural power which Hindus call *Parmatma* and also its reflection or micro-scopic part which they call *Atma.* They have no other explanation of death except that *Atma,* or light, or energy has gone out of the body. Indian education should, in keeping with our culture, teach students about this spirit, especially that matter is not lasting but *Atma* is, that love of *Atma* will lead to *Anand, i.e*, permanent happiness, that the aim of life is to get *Moksha, i.e.*, freedom from the bondage of the cycle of birth and death, etc.

Thus, the aim of the Indian education, in keeping with our old culture, civilization, value-system should be to help the students, as per their capacities, in developing physically, intellectually, morally, spiritually and making them useful citizens of the country and the world. In other words to develop their personality in an integrated and balanced way. It is a wrong concept that only good results make an institutions elite. Even if the academic results are not very good but the average students has a balanced, developed and integrated personality, the institution has done its job. It is undoubtedly a very good institution.

The Goals

Once a Principal knows his infrastructure and resources and is also aware of the ultimate goals to be achieved and the direction in which to move, then it shall not be difficult to fix up the goals for the institution. Unfortunately, today, extra stress is laid on the examination results. If an institution is able to give good results, both numerically and qualitatively, it is considered an elite school or college. But this is not correct. A good institution should be able to bring about an all round development of its students. To this end, the Principal should work. For example, if in the institution, the Examination results are good but no facilities exist for games, N.C.C., Scouting or for extra-curricular activities as debates, cultural programmes, etc., or the students do not participate in them, then the college cannot be called a good one. It cannot develop a balance personality of its students. In such a situation, the Principal's first priority should be to provide maximum facilities to improve physical fitness of an average students and also his other talents. The present practice to pick up only a few dozen students is no good. This may demonstrate the world that the college is good in games and extra curricular activities but the reality will be some what different. So, each and every student must be first made conscious of the need of being physically fit, then of the essentials of how to become healthy, and thereafter, the facilities be provided and a taste for each activity be developed. It is not a one day job and needs lot of planning and efforts.

Again, if the students are good in studies, games and extra curricular activities but lack in discipline, or do not possess sweet manners, or do not know how to smartly dress, how to gracefully walk, how to influence people by their talk, or are deficient in general knowledge and worldly affairs, then the college cannot be called elite. The principal must give priority to these matters and plan the ways and means to overcome these deficiencies of the students. He can, for example, use Dale Cornale's books, 'How to make friends and Influence people', Indianise the contents, and organise lectures in each class, at least once a week. He has also to ensure that students follow these guide lines in their own life. Today, glitter sells.

Today, a situation has developed when most of the students do not know the meaning of the Indian values of life, viz, truth, simplicity, love, non-violence, self-control, non-Anger, patriotism, etc. It is the duty of a college to make its students moral oriented. so, meaning of these values, the advantages of imbibing them in life and how can they be imbibed be told to the students. Some strategies should be invented and experiments made to popularise these values.

Patriotism is the Master solution of our several multi-faceted problems. Unfortunately, in the post-independence period, patriotism has become a casualty. It is the duty of a Principal to make his students patrioritic. They must be taught the history, geography, culture, value-system, and life and achievements of the greatmen of the country, etc., in correct perspective. False history should have no place in lessons of patriotism. Patriotism means not only loving the

3

OFFICE PLANNING AND CONTROLLING

The office of the Principal is eyes, brain and heart of an institution. On its efficient functioning depends the present and future of the institution. It is a place where records for the purpose or information and efficient operation are prepared, handled and preserved. It is, therefore essential to have an efficient office with a systematic, fool proof and stable working pattern.

It is unfortunate that in India no studies of college offices have been scientifically undertaken and guidelines given to improve administration. So, an attempt is being made here, on the basis of personal experience, exchange of views with other Principals and the study undertaken by the Administrative Staff College of India, Hyderabad of the University of Poona.

I.
LOCATE SHORTCOMINGS

The Principal should keep a close watch on the existing set-up and functioning of his office to identify the short-comings. It is likely, that he may find out the following shortcomings.

a) *Office Building, Furniture and Equipment:* It is likely that the Principal's room and his office may not be located in one buildings. It is also possible that the building may not be airy, well ventilated and safe. In all possibilities the working space may not be sufficient, or its use may not be optimal. Similarly, the furniture may be ricketty and untidy and equipment may be old, outdated or insufficient. All this hampers efficiency.

b) *Lack of Proper Sectioning of Office:* A Principal may discover that his office has not been properly divided into separate sections of units like Accounts, General office, Statistical Section, Machine Section, Building Section etc. It hinders efficient disposal of office work and creates confusion.

c) *Continuation of irrelevant methods:* Normally, a Principal takes the line of least resistance and follows the same methods and procedures which have been in practice for several years. Some of them must have certainly become out of date or irrelevant because of the continuous changes—students number, variety of subjects, new classes, new schemes introduced by U.G.C., Central Government and State Government etc. For example, the old method was to preserve yearly records for which lot of space was needed. Now this work can be entrusted to computer and space and time can be economised.

d) *Grouping of unrelated activities:* The Principal may find out that the existing working units (branches) of the college administration are not based on any established rational principle of scientific management. The existing set up is based on convenience and trial and error method. Hence a number of unrelated activities constitute a working unit while a number of related activities are attached to different working units. This leads to delay and increase in work load.

e) *Wrong staffing:* The Principal may find out that in the absence of work studies of each and every table, some units or branches of the office are over-staffed while others are under staffed. This may lead to inefficiency and delay and dissatisfaction among overloaded staff.

f) *Defective placing and lack of training:* Every one cannot do every thing with equal efficiency. So, the selection, placement and training assumes importance. Normally very little attention is paid to this aspect. It is neglected in colleges.

g) *Lack of clarity in duties and responsibilities:* Normally a worker is not given a duty chart — what work he has to do. In the absence of this duty chart, he is called upon to attend to any duty which his superior wants to entrust him on a particular day. This, on the one hand, leads to mistakes and inefficiency because the worker will take time to understand this new job and on the other hand, makes none accountable for mistakes.

This lack of proper distribution of work becomes more pronounced in the case of supervisory staff. Normally, a file passes through a number of incharges before finally reaching the Principal. This is unnecessary duplication and waste of time and energy.

h) *Lack of decision-taking at different levels:* The Principal may find out, much to his chagrin, that none wants to take responsibility of taking a decision even on routine matters. All pass on the buck to higher ones. This increases paper work and delays in decision-taking. This also generates an unrealistic feeling amongst the staff that there is too much work. The Principal is also loaded with lot of routine work with hardly any time left for policy decisions and forward planning etc.

i) *Absence of co-ordination:* It is to be investigated whether the required level of coordination exists between different units or sections of the office. Normally, there is a lack of coordination as each unit thinks itself to be independent and superior to the other. The result is that the time schedules are not adhered to.

j) *Absence of Public Relations:* Normally, an institution has no public relation activity. There is not even a separate Enquiry office where students, teachers and parents can get required informations. This means that various section incharges or Principal are disturbed. This is not good. Further, in the modern world, no institution can progress without sympathy and support from public and government. A sense of belonging should be developed in different segments connected with a college. A good public relation system will deliver the goods.

k) *Lack of clear-cut notings, decisions and proper drafting:* So often decisions are taken just on the basis of half-half and oral report on a case given by the dealing assistant or other responsible person. Proper noting of the case history and issue involved is not made. This, so often, makes the decisions erroneous. Then, the decisions taken are generally not exhaustive. They lack clarity and much is left to be understood. They are also not properly drafted. It creates confusion and opens doors to litigation.

l) *Absence of planning:* A college, to be able to achieved its goals, should have proper Planning and its efficient execution. Normally planning should mean fixing targets, analysing resources, placing them in an ideal combination so as to achieve the desired results in the shortest possible time. This also means proper control and direction.

m) *Return of papers to applicant:* Normally, a Principal returns the papers after passing order, to the applicant with a view that it may be given to the person concerned. It should never be done.

II.
HOW TO ORGANISE THE OFFICE

The Principal, after identifying the shortcomings of office set-up and working should proceed to correct them. Here are some broad ideas:

1. Office Building

The Principal's office should be, as far as possible, located near the entrance gate. It is a wrong idea to locate it in a far off corner or even at a central place. It must be an independent building. The building must be well protected against sudden out-bursts of violence.

To make the building airy and well ventilated, efforts be made to provide big windows and ventilators. However, these windows and ventilators should have iron grills.

The Accounts section should be given a separate hall with only one strong entrance gate. The counters should open in covered big varandah so that students may be protected from sun and rain. The fee clerks, counters should be at one end of the Hall and they should be further protected with inside grills. The Accountant's office should be at the entrance closely followed by the cashiers table and there after should be seated other clerks of accounts sections. There should be a small attached store with lots of racks to keep records safely. One gate, near the accountant, should open in the Principal's room.

The other hall should be given to the General Section. Its one gate should open in the Principal's room. It should have minimum doors so that students of outsiders may not have easy access inside the Hall. Like the Accounts section, the General Section Hall should have a counter at one end of it with a covered verandah outside.

2. The Office Furniture

The office furniture should have several characteristics, viz.

a) It should be of good quality and well maintained.
b) It should economise space and also provide space where each office hand can safely keep his running records under lock and key. For example, a table-cum-almirah can be designed. The

ability. Only when the Principal and teachers become aware of the weaknesses and merits of students that it will be possible to prepare strategy to help them achieve excellence. Here both the macro and micro approaches will be required.

2. The Principal should have a clear idea about the faculty members, their competence both of subject matter and communication ability, the degree of motivation they have, the love they have for students, their devotion and sincerity towards profession, self-discipline, self-studies, etc. When an indepth fact finding is done, several appalling facts will come to knowledge. There are more than 10 per cent teachers who do not regularly go to their classes and this number is on the increase. Most of the teachers gossip in practicals. Bulk of teachers do not keep themselves abreast with the latest developments in their subjects. Their knowledge is 20-25 year old. The teachers just try to cover the courses without caring to know how much has been grasped by the average students. They do not encourage students to put questions, rather snub them when they take such an initiative. A teacher may have a good reputation but he may not be planning his courses will. He may be laying undue stress on one or two units in which he himself is good and may be skipping over the other units.
3. The Principal should know about the college library and plan it so as to meet the new requirements. Today, college libraries have not the latest Journals and Reference material. They can hardly afford them. As an alternative they do not even subscribe for Abstracts of subject – Journals which give the summary of latest development and are a good substitute to costly books and journals. The whole library needs planning.
4. The Principal should know the infrastructure of the college. Without an efficient and sufficient infrastructure nothing material can be achieved.

After equipping himself about the students, the teachers, the library and the infrastructure, the Principal should cautiously take the following steps:

1. **Admissions**

A Principal cannot refuse admissions on the basis of sex, caste, colour, rural or urban domicile, wealth, educational background of the family, etc. What he can do is to fix number of admissions, classwise, in conformity with the rules and regulations of the university such as number of students in one section (take the lower limit), workload of teachers, etc. He must also take into consideration the number of class rooms, their sizes, the furniture, etc. He cannot also ignore the sizes of the laboratories while deciding about the number of students to be admitted in practical subjects. He must remember that when emphasis turns to quantity, quality becomes the first casualty.

The Principal should also declare that admissions will be given on the basis of merit. And the merit will be quantified on the basis of the past academic records, achievements in extra-curricular activities, etc. This quantification should also judiciously provide for negative marks for indiscipline, a criminal case pending in a court, failure, time-gap etc.

The Principal should try to do one thing more. Every college has its catchment areas. Quite an appreciable number of students seek admission to the college from two, three nearby institutions. They must be identified. The Principal should try to establish contact with the Principals of and members of the Managing Committees of these colleges and should impress upon them the need to take steps to make their respective colleges quality oriented. What they should do and what they should avoid be told to them in mutual exchange of views. It is like admitting students from convent schools or trying to make an ordinary school akin to a convent school (see Chapter on Admissions).

2. The Principal should properly organize college Library and should make it a place of intensive self-study. (See Chapter on Library Re-organisation).
3. The Principal should request the teaches to divide the course — Contents of each subject of each class into the following components:

   a) Which topics are to be covered by lecture method. Here syllabus will have to be UNITISED and teaching-learning process will have to be used.
   b) Which topics will be covered through library assignments. It must be remembered that today library is the most important

single factor for excellence. In the western world students suck 80 per cent knowledge from the library and the remaining 20 per cent from teachers. Students, therefore, must be asked to review, say, ten books, or ten journals. They must also be requested to read two topics from the Abstracts of subject journals giving the latest developments and reproduce them before other classmates.

c) Which topics will be covered through discussions.

d) Which topics will be covered through project work.

The teachers must be persuaded to adopt all these four methods so that students' command over latest strides in knowledge may increase and their analytical and critical ability may develop.

4. The teachers need brush up their own knowledge of the subject and to acquire the latest techniques of teaching. They need exposures at regular intervals. The U.G.C. has established, at different university centres, the Academic Staff College where regular refresher courses for subject teachers are held. The Principal should arrange to send his teachers, to these Staff Colleges. Besides this, he should motivate them to improve their academic qualifications and contribute articles to subject journals. He should provide facilities to them to attend conferences and contribute papers. The Principal should also persuade teachers to apply for Research Grants and establish contacts with the separate Research Institutions and information centres (see Chapter on Funding Agencies).
5. The weaknesses of students must be identified and they should be helped in overcoming them through special coaching, etc. It will be a good idea that a teacher gives a short test in his class, once a month. Records of results of each student should be maintained. This will show the successive progression of a student — is he stationary, improving or going down? Thereafter remedial measures may be taken.

Real excellence will go up when average excellence increases. Further, all students will not exceed either in all things or in common things. Different students may excel in different spheres. For example, students from rural areas may excel in sports or may be creative story writers or good poets or good observers. Similarly, city dwellers may be good organisers, good at studies, or good in general knowledge. So, it is essential to know the students' interests and mould them accordingly.

The success or failure of the Principal's efforts to improve the academic atmosphere of his college will mainly depend upon the following factors:

1. Cooperation from the Managing Committee of the College, specially the college Secretary. Normally, it is very unlikely to get support from them.
2. The reduction in number of students admitted. Quantity and quality do not go together.
3. The cooperation from teachers. Today a situation has developed in which 10 per cent teachers are likely to be actively with the Principal in whatever he chooses to do. Another 10 per cent are likely to be in the opposition camp just because they are work shirkers and anti-administration. The rest of 80 per cent sit on the fence. They need motivation. This calls upon the Principals qualities of leadership and powers to motivate these teachers. If he is able to generate a sense of belonging amongst the teachers, non-teachers and students, he is bound to succeed.
4. The college should have a well organised, efficient and well equipped infrastructure. Much cannot be achieved without it. So, the Principal should pay special attention to infrastructure, before taking any steps to make the institution an elite one.

country's territory, but also respecting and loving its culture, value-system and the greatmen and to be prepared to sacrifice even life in protecting them. Just as love for extra-territorial loyalties is an un-patriotic act, similarly, unthought out adoption of other country's culture, value-system and greatmen is treachery.

Suppose the college results are poor. How to improve the academic life? The Principal should try to investigate and find out the cases of poor results. Are the teachers not taking classes regularly or teaching properly? Is the students' background poor and are they not able to follow lectures? Are the teaching days not sufficient? Has the institution not sufficient class rooms and furniture and so classes are over crowded? Are the students not sufficiently reading at home? If so, why? Once the causes and their priorities are known, efforts must be made to tackle them, one by one, with the available means.

Thus, a Principal, should try to pay heed to the fact that the institution should make an intensive effort for an all round development of its students with its means.

One thing needs special mentioning here. Much can be easily achieved in a very short period if a sense of belonging to and pride for the institution can be developed amongst students and teachers and non-teachers of the college. A successful Principal, through his actions and speeches much be able to develop such sentiments.

Future Growth

An institution should not remain static as far as its growth is concerned. Today, most of the institutions add classes and subjects without any serious thought. The wrong idea is that the greater the number of subjects, classes, students, teachers and non-teachers, *i.e.*, the empire, the bigger the college and the better. This is not correct idea.

The University Grants Commission gave the posts of a "Director of College Development" to most of the Affiliating Universities. My impression is that very good people have been asked to man these posts but they have hardly developed a line of thinking and philosophy on the directions of the future growth of the colleges. Similarly, the university and the Government have no expertise in the matter. So, colleges develop in an unplanned way. A good Principal must not do it. He must know, in these days of specialisation, what subjects or classes to add to make it a compact college capable of giving specialised services to the community in the sphere the services are required most. For example, the district of Aligarh is primarily an agricultural district. Is it not shocking that in the district, not a single institution, including the Aligarh Muslim University, has an agricultural college or subjects connected with agriculture at B.A./B.Sc. or M.A./M.Sc. level.

So, the decision of the direction in which an institution should be made to develop, should be taken carefully. The educational institutions' primary role is to serve the community by producing capable end-products, who can deliver the goods. And, in the process to help the students also. So the decision on growth should weigh with these two primary considerations.

2

PLANNING FOR ACADEMIC EXCELLENCE

One of the primary functions of a Principal is to plan for academic excellence. The Principal's function is not limited to the extent of keeping the college running. That is really no job. That way the college can run even without any Principal. The Principal must be dynamic enough to steer the college on the vertical path of academic excellence. So, it is essential to know the meaning of academic excellence in the modern context before planning to achieve it.

Meaning of Excellence

Today, the horizons of knowledge are expanding very fast. The store of knowledge almost doubles in five years. In earlier days, when knowledge was not expanding that fast ideas first came in books and then they were propagated further and put in use. Now they first appear in journals, their propagation and use starts right then, they appear in books only at a later stage.

So, excellence in a subject or a combination of subjects entails that an average student should be able to lay his hands on journals highlighting the latest developments in various branches of knowledge even before they appear in books.

The second constituent of excellence is the ability to reproduce in a better way, what a student has read.

Another significant constituent of excellence is to have good general knowledge, besides the knowledge of subjects — courses and have a general awareness of the changes that are taking place in India and abroad.

The Government talks of *'Equality of opportunity'* in matters of education. It simply means that a student is not discriminated on any ground, in admission. It is a known fact that intellectual sharpness and achievements of a student positively have a co-relation with his family background and the environment from which he comes up.

For example, rural students are not as bright as urban students. Similarly, students from poor families are not as bright as those from middle class or rich families. So, today to restrict admissions only for bright students and thereby automatically have excellent results is not possible. That can also not be the proper measure of a good institution. Today, equality of opportunity also implies *'equality in output'*. An excellent institution is one which is able to bridge this inequality in output. This is possible only when additional support is provided to weak students. The U.G.C. has started Remedial Courses with this end in view.

It is not enough that a student accumulates readymade knowledge and disgorges it on his examination desk. It is essential that a student digests what he learns and develops a critical faculty so that he may be able to understand, analyse, and apply this knowledge profitably. In other words, he must develop a scientific mind.

Today, gaining knowledge is no more considered to be an end in itself. It is required to promote local, social and national interests and welfare. So, the question of excellence is now related with development. A new concept is developing that an educational institution should contribute to solving the local problems of industry, agriculture, trade, transport, etc., and thereby help in the development of the area. In U.S.A. Community Colleges were established with this end in mind. Recently, the U.G.C. has come out with the scheme of autonomous colleges in India.

Academic excellence, therefore, means acquiring subject knowledge with the same pace with which it is expanding, to have general awareness, to develop a scientific temper, to have not only equality of opportunity in admissions but also equality in output and to apply it to the good of the society and the humanity at large.

How to Achieve it?

To be able to achieved something the Principal should know his grounds well. So:

1. The Principal, as far as possible, should try to know his students. He must know their socio-politico-economic and educational background. He must also know their language competence and competence levels of subjects. Today examination grades are not the correct indicator of a student's

door of the almirah should be collapsible to become the table-top.

c) As far as possible, separate table-chair be provided to each office-hand.

3. The Office Equipment

The tools and efficiency are directly related. Hence, good quality of pen, paper, ink, type-writers, both Hindi and English, calculators, photostat machine (not duplicating machine), Inter-communication system and computer be provided to office. Today computers can be put to several remarkable uses:

a) To prepare Salary Bills. It will be a good idea if the salary statement of each employee is provided to him each month showing his Basic Salary, D.A., House Allowance, etc., and deduction of Income Tax, P.F., etc.
b) To prepare monthly income – expenditure statement.
c) To prepare Bank Reconciliation statement.
d) To prepare list of candidates — classwise in an Alphabetical order with their bio-data.
e) Preservation of Files and other materials.

Today, U.G.C. is freely giving computer to colleges.

It will be good idea to instal a siren with its speaker units facing different direction instead of a manually operated bell. It can be set to automatically give one short whistle after the end of each period of say 40 mts. or 45 mts. of 60 mts. as the case may be.

4. Sections or Units

The number of office units should depend upon the work load. Normally, for a college with a strength of less than 1.5 thousand students the following units can be proposed:

a) Reception
b) General
c) Accounts
d) Statistical, Inspection, affiliation, G.O.'s.

And for a big college, the following units will be better:

a) Reception, Public Relations and Publications.
b) General
c) Accounts
d) Building
e) Typing and Machine Unit
f) Examination
g) Statistical, Inspection, affiliation, G.O.'s.

As per resources, these units can be clubbed together or more independent units can be formed.

5. Supervisory Staff

Each section or unit must be put under an Incharge. The senior most of the section can be made Incharge.

The Bursar should be incharge of the Accounts Section. If there is no Bursar, then the Head Clerk or Office Superintendent must look after the work of Accounts Section also.

The Office-Superintendent or Head Clerk must be overall incharge of all other sections.

All papers, other than those of routine nature that are placed before the Principal must invariably pass through the Office Superintendent or the Bursar as the case may be.

The Office Superintendent or the Bursar should ensure that detailed noting is provided for the information of the Principal. All vital matters involving policy decision should move with the whole file and comprehensive noting. This will enable the Principal to know facts and law and also check them up from file.

6. Strength of Staff

The Director of Higher Education, U.P, has laid down norms of the staff for the Principal's office. They, with slight modifications may be adopted.

The Directorate of Higher Education has provided one Assistant for every 200 students. This is in addition to the posts of Bursar, Office Suprintendent, Accountant and Steno.

7. Selection, Placement and Training

The Principal must try to assess the capabilities and aptitudes, etc., of the members of his office staff. It must be admitted that every one cannot be good at figure work. Some are of course exceedingly good at such work. So, job studies may be done in a rough way. Then through personal interview method, the work aptitudes and worker's own assessment about him-self be known. After this, each staff member be given a seat.

After placement, the office hand must be helped to understand and pick-up the work. Somebody must guide him. This may be called a training period. The duration of this training period will depend upon the nature of work at that table and the capabilities of the worker.

The Principal must keep himself informed, through Incharge and other means, of the quality and quantity of output. If it is less than desired, the change of seat may be tried.

It will be good policy if more than one person is trained to handle the work at each table. It will break monopoly of the worker and consequently his likely bad temper. Moreover, the section Incharge must allot the quantum of Non-recurring work to each table each day and ensure that it is completed on day-to-day basis besides disposal of the recurring routine work at the table.

8. Duty Chart

The Incharges of different sections must be asked to prepare Duty charts for each table. Further, recurring work should not be clubbed with no-recurring work such as submission of examination forms, statistics, processing of students records, posting of service books, preparation of college Budget, etc. The allied works must be grouped together for each table.

9. Motivation

The most important thing, but generally the least valued, is motivation of the staff. Today, if a Principal wants to maintain a relationship of a boss and subordinate and displays snobbery, it will not help in making the institute elite. So, the relationship should be that of a family and the Principal should play the role of the head of the family or a leader of the team. He should know the individuals by name, their family problems, if any, and help in solving such problems mainly through sympathy and advice and sometimes even through resources. This equation pays rich dividends and helps in minimising strikes, agitations, "work to rule", etc.

One thing more. A sense of belonging to the institution and pride in the institution, go a long way in ensuring efficiency. This motivation can be provided by the Principal through his own actions and also repeatedly talking with the workers, individually and collectively. The whole idea should be drilled in every body's mind.

10. Office Records

(A) *General Section*

Besides the files and registers of routine nature that may be needed from time time, the general section must maintain the following permanent records:

(i) *Personal files of staff:* Every personal file must begin with a copy of the advertisement for the post and must contain all initial papers such as application of the incumbent, a copy of synopsis of applications, authority of appointment, e.g., recommendation of the Selection Committee or the Commission and the Management's resolution, appointment letter, approval by the Vice-Chancellor/DDR/ DIOS, etc. and then all papers of permanent importance, relating to the incumbent should be placed on the personal file. The personal files should contain an index. Every page of it should be numbered.

(ii) *Service Books:* A service book is a synopsis of the personal file. Service books are maintained in approved printed form. They should be completed annually. In cases where an employee makes some achievement like an additional qualification or an award, entry in the service book should be made immediately, putting the supporting paper on the personal file.

(iii) *Students' admissions file:* Students admission forms classwise may be preserved in guard files yearwise.

(iv) *Students admission register and S.R. register:* Students admission register provides ready information about the students, particularly their local and permanent addresses. A new admission register is prepared every year and it is useful record for finding the addresses of students.

The admission register being change every year fails to provide a running record of a student during the entire period of his stay in the college. When a student of say four year's standing comes to take a character certificate or his record is demanded for Government service, etc. four years admission registers have to be referred to. For ready information S.R. registers need be maintained. S.R. number may be allotted to a student as he first enters on the college rolls. The first two digits of this number may denote the year of his admission. This S.R. form may have columns for years, classes, examination results, and other positive or negative achievements of a student.

(v) *Affiliation files:* These files must be maintained very systematically. The file should be able to provide a comprehensive picture of the process of an affiliation through the different phases. It will be advisable to have an abstract of affiliation conditions of each class, subjectwise, and ensure that they are observed.

(vi) *Inspection files:* Like the affiliation files the inspection files should also be maintained carefully.

(vii) *Statistics registers:* Frequently, the state and central governments and the Directorate of Education ask for detailed statistics regarding students, teachers, and other establishment. The U.G.C. also asks for statistics on a wide canvas while inviting applications for grants. Much time is wasted and much tension piles up when statistics are compiled at the time of their submission. It is, therefore, necessary to prepare year-wise statistics in five registers separately for students, teachers, research scholars, library and finances.

(a) The classwise data of students prepared every year may cover the following information in two groups: (i) at the time of admission, and (ii) at the time of taking the Examination. Every item of information may be sub-divided into two parts — Boys and Girls: The items can be

Total No.

No. of S.C.

No. of S.T.
No. of B.C.
General

Break up in Age groups — 16 to 30 years with intervals of 5 years with Rural and Urban
Exam. Result I Div., II Div., III Div., Percentage.

(b) The statistics about teachers may cover the following information:

No. .... Department-wise
Total No.
Total No. of D. Litt./D.Scs.
Total No. of Ph.Ds.
Break up — Grade-wise
Work load on teachers — Department-wise

(c) The Research Register may contain yearwise names of scholars registered with topics and names of Research guides. It should also contain details of scholars working with U.G.C., C.S.I.R. or other grants. Awards of Ph.Ds., subject-wise, be also recorded in this register. It will be better if this Register is made Research-Guide-wise. All the Ph.D. students of a teacher be recorded on one sheet.

(d) The statistics register for library will provide such information as:

Total No. of Books : Gen. library and Book bank
No. of papers & Magazine
subscribed — Daily, Weekly, Fortnightly, Monthly, Quarterly
No. of Books floated in circulation
No. of student benefited
No. of teachers benefited
No. of Research scholars benefited
Amount of Books spent during the

year on Books, Magazines etc.

(e) The statistics regarding finance will show actuals of expenditure on different budget heads — Recurring and Non-recurring.

(viii) *Times table files:* The General section will maintain three types of time tables for each year — classwise, teacher — wise and roomwise. The teacherwise time table will also show the load of work of every teacher.

(ix) *Stock books:* the stock books of furniture, electricity, office, *etc.,* are to be maintained by the office. The furniture stock book must show the entire furniture of the college, and its distribution in class rooms, laboratories, departments and offices and the balance in the godown. Similar is to be the case with non-consumable articles of electricity. The consumable items may be shown as "fitted at . . . . . place". And so of office machines.

(x) *G.O.'s and circulars file:* All G.Os and circulars — of general nature should be put in a separate file, in original. This file must be maintained by the Office Superintendent. Copies of the G.Os and circulars, attested by the Principal should be sent to the dealing assistants and all the other sections and departments concerned. It will be better if copies of G.Os concerning teachers be sent to the Secretary, Staff Association. Similarly, G.Os relating to accounts and finances should be maintained in a separate file by the Bursar or the O.S., as the case may be. It is essential that the latest position should clearly be recorded.

(xi) *Record of leave:* This record should also be accurately maintained. Applications for casual leave may be kept in a general file but all other type of leave applications having provision of being accumulated should be put on personal files of Staff. Account of all type of leave should be kept in a register and be posted in the individual service books year to year.

(xii) *Examination files:* Besides the different files to be prepared by the Examination Central Office, the general office of the college will maintain the following record related to examinations.

1. Consolidated statement of absentees.
2. Classwise details of students caught using unfair means.
3. Circulars of the university concerning decisions of cases of unfair means.
4. Roll lists.
5. Result books received from the university.
6. Marks sheets of students (carbon copies) which may be got bound yearwise for proper maintenancc.

(B) *Account Section*

This is rather a sensitive section of a college office since the slightest inadvertent error may lead to unimaginable complications. As far as possible, the accounts work should be done on prescribed forms. There are bound volumes available of cash books, abstract registers, fee charged and provident fund and scholarship registers, income-tax and fee concession and all such other registers as electricity consumption and water consumption a/c, advance paid, etc. Posting of accounts particularly of the cash books and abstract registers should be done everyday. Bank reconciliation statements should be prepared every month to verify and tally the balance in the Bank and on record in cash books.

Advance accounts be reconciled every month. Notices be given to the persons who have not submitted account of advances made to them.

Printed forms also should be used for procuring sanctions, preparing comparative statements of quotations and placing orders, cash book vouchers before making payments, transferring individual salary to Bank, etc.

The accounts section should also maintain the following files:

a) G.Os and circulars relating to accounts
b) Sanctions of renewal of creation on posts
c) Matters related to Provident fund and Income tax of teachers and others
d) Pensions
e) Scholarships
f) Pending Bills
g) Vouchers

h) Audit reports
i) Salary Bills
j) Returns submitted to the Directorate and other authorities.

These are some important files. There may be many more. Every college should adopt some set account rules which should be exhaustive and made known to all sections and departments of the college for strict adherence. When the account sections finds something wanting in a set of account papers and refers them back to the concerned department, long note will not be necessary. Only reference to Rule No. will suffice.

Common with the General and Accounts Section : Inward Dak Register

This register may be maintained by the steno or the P.A. Besides the usual columns of particulars of letters, it should also have columns for the name of the dealing Asstt., the time given to him for disposal and the time of actual disposal alongwith its reference.

All this is to be noted on the impression of a rubber stamp to be affixed on incoming letters;

Sl. No ....
Date of receipt ....
File No.. ......
Date of disposal..... ..
Reference No.. ....Date.........

The steno/P.A. should put before the Principal a weekly report of the papers that have not been disposed of in time.

Outward Dak Register

This register besides the usual columns should have a columns for file No. The number marked on the outgoing letters should be as follows:

S.No. of Dak Register	File No.	Session
e.g. 532/A-3/87-88		

Filing

In the modern days of advanced technology, many efficient systems of filing are available. A college may adopt any one of them. The aim, however, should be to make a reference available immediately at call without unnecessary wastage of time. Papers should be filed promptly. If once they get dumped, it becomes difficult to file them and a vicious circle forms.

4

THE COLLEGE ACCOUNTS

Very few Principals know even the basic rudiments of accounts. It is, essential for every Principal to know :

1. Why the Accounts are maintained.
2. Methods to maintain Accounts.
3. Main books of Accounts.
4. Accounts procedures and various proformas.
5. The college Budget and the under-lying policy.
6. Financial Control.

It will be advisable to take up these points one by one.

I. WHY THE ACCOUNTS

In ancient times, the daily transactions of a person or even a shop or workshop were very limited and a person could remember them, therefore the necessity of maintaining proper accounts was not felt. The idea of future projections and planning for future was also missing. So neither daily accounts were written nor any account books maintained. However, as the business and production increased and institutions assumed larger proportions it became very difficult to remember each and every item of income and expenditure and, therefore, it became necessary to record the various items of income and expenditure. This is how the accounts and the art of preparing accounts were born. With the passage of time and the increase in complexity of transactions, different types of account books and different methods of accounting were evolved.

Accounting, which is a also referred to as book keeping, is a science and an art by which income-expenditure and other transactions of an establishment are recorded in certain book in a certain way regularly. Book keeping is not difficult to learn. Anyone with an aptitude for figure work can do it with some training.

However, one thing is certain that today accounting is an integral part of every establishment having financial transactions. It is as important as any other function. The main functions which accounting serves are :

1. Keeping systematic record of all financial transactions.
2. Protecting properties of the establishment (through proper control and reconciliations).
3. Communicating the results of business to investors, employees, owners government, etc., for the purpose of planning and controls. In other establishments, it helps assessment of the financial position.

It may be opined that an educational institution is not a business proposition. So, why so much importance to its account? In today's materialistic world everything has became money oriented. It has become essential to even maintain accounts of home. And then in a college, money comes from students, government, U.G.C., donors, etc. They all want to ensure that their money is properly utilised. For future planning also, it is necessary to keep accounts systematically.

II.
METHOD OF MAINTAINING ACCOUNTS

There are two methods of systems of preparing accounts — The Single Entry System and The Double Entry System.

It will be advisable to know something about both the systems.

The Single Entry System

The Single Entry System of Book keeping is really no system though it is economical. There are no set rules for maintaining accounts under this system. People generally maintain personal accounts and cash books under this system. Prof. J.R. Batliboi defines the single entry system as 'one in which personal accounts of debtors and creditors are maintained. Sometimes, subsidiary books are also maintained as in the Double Entry system but in them too only those postings are made which have reference to personal accounts . . . it is double entry system in incomplete form.'

In the Single Entry System, a cash book is maintained in which only the cash transactions are entered. Ledgers are also maintained but in them , only the accounts of creditors are shown. Subsidiary books such as the Purchases Book, Purchases Returns Book, Bill payable Book, etc., are generally not maintained and, if maintained, only the personal accounts are posted in different ledgers from the subsidiary books.

Demerits of the Single Entry System

1. Importance is given only to personal accounts. Impersonal Accounts are not put on relevant ledgers with the result that full knowledge about the accounts cannot to obtained.
2. This system doses not admit of preparation of Trial Balance since of the two forms of a transaction, only one form is posted in the Account Books. So mathematical accuracy of the accounts cannot be ascertained.
3. Actual financial position of any fund cannot be ascertained.
4. Useful statistics of the accounts is not available without going through a long compilation work.
5. Errors cannot be detected so easily as they can be detected in the Double Entry System.
6. Verification of accuracy of accounts is not only difficult but also almost impossible. Hence there are chances of misappropriations and embezzlements.

   For all these demerits, the Single Entry System is considered incomplete, unscientific and unreliable. On the contrary, the double entry system is considered complete, scientific and reliable.

The Double Entry System

The Double Entry System of Book keeping is based on the assumption that every financial transactions has two aspects — the debit and the credit. Every debit aspect has its credit aspect and the vice versa. In the Double Entry System, both these aspects are duly posted and that is why it is called the Double Entry system. The debit and credit aspects of a transaction are recorded on the basis of certain principles, a preliminary idea of which will be given later on in this chapter.

Characteristics of Double Entry System

1. *It is judicious:* When a transaction is gone through (whether related to sale and purchase or receipt-payment of cash), two sides are involved in it, i.e., every transaction has two aspects. In this system both the aspects are posted in Account Books and that is judicious. If only one aspect is recorded and the other ignored, the account will not be accurate and proper.
2. *It records personal as well as impersonal aspects:* May be that both the aspects of a transaction are personal, or both of them impersonal or one of them personal and the other impersonal. The Double Entry System records both the aspects and that is why it is considered to be more scientific.
3. *Postings made on the basis of set rules:* Although in this system, one aspect of a transaction is called debit and the other credit but that does not mean that randomly either of the aspects is recorded as 'Debit' and the other 'credit'. There are set rules for doing so.
4. *Helpful in ascertaining mathematical accuracy:* Since one aspect of every transaction is debit and the other credit, the totals of the debit and the credit sides must tally. This comparisons gives an ideal of mathematical accuracy of accounts. This accuracy is ascertained through Trial Balance.

Rules for Ascertaining the Debit and Credit Aspects of a Transaction

Accounts are broadly of the following types :

1. *Personal Accounts:* Accounts that are opened with relation to individuals, firms, institutions, companies, corporations, etc., are called personal accounts.
2. *Impersonal Accounts:* They have two parts —

   (a) *Real Accounts:* Accounts related to properties and titles are called Real Accounts, e.g., Building A/c, Cash A/c. Furniture A/c, Science Equipment A/c. etc.

   (b) *Nominal Accounts:* All accounts allied to income and expenditure are called Nominal Accounts, *e.g.,* Salary A/c, Rent A/c, Interest A/c, etc.

Coming to rules of debit and credit entries, it is prescribed that —

1. In cases of personal accounts, the "Receiver" is debited and the "Giver" is credited.
2. In cases of Real Accounts, the thing that 'comes is debited and that which 'goes out' is credited.
3. In cases of nominal accounts, the 'Expenses and losses' are debited while the 'Income and Profit Accounts are credited'.

These rules can be applied as such even when the two aspects of a transaction refer to two different types of accounts — personal and impersonal.

The Double Entry System is a bit technical and requires trained staff for its maintenance. *It is , however, advisable that in colleges, the Double Entry system should be adopted to ensure a fool-proof and perfect maintenance of Accounts.*

III.
MAIN BOOKS OF ACCOUNT

It will be desirable to have some idea of the various Books of Accounts and important basic documents.

Vouchers: The basic documents or papers on which a transaction originates are called vouchers. A voucher is a documentary evidence in support of a transaction, the voucher can be a in any form, e.g., the bill for purchases made, the invoice for sales made, the receipt for amounts collected, the receipts for amounts paid, etc. On the basis of these vouchers it is decided which account is to be debited and which account to be credited. Some business houses, for the sake of convenience and for accuracy, print formats for vouchers and on the basis of documents mentioned above, those printed formats are filled in and are then used as vouchers for recording entries in books.

In case of cash transactions, since one head is always cash, therefore in order to simplify the recording, separate vouchers for cash payments and cash receipts are made which are called debit and credit vouchers respectively; and for transactions where heads other than cash are affected, other vouchers generally known as Journal vouchers are used.

On the basis of these vouchers books of account are maintained.

Books of Accounts: The principal books of account are : Memorandum Book, Journal (in case of Double Entry System), Cash Book and Ledger. The details of these books may be summarised as follows :

Memorandum Book or West Book: It is a sort of range book in which a transaction is noted immediately as and when it occurs so as to ensure that all transactions are duly posted in relevant account books. The Memorandum Books is, however, not an essential account book.

Journal

The process of book-keeping in Double Entry System of accounts starts with the journal. It is the base book from which further entries of accounts in the cash book, the Ledgers and other subsidiary books are made. The journal has a definite format. The following illustration shows the format of a journal and the way of posting transaction in it.

Transactions

Oct. 1 : Purchased Books on Bill from Jagrati Book Centre — Rs. 3000

Oct. 3 : Purchased stationery on cash payment — Rs. 2000

Oct. 4 : Paid salaries to Non-Teaching Staff — Rs. 25,000

Oct. 7 : Deposited Rs. 50,000 in Bank.

Entries in the Journal

Date	Particulars	L.F.	Amount Dr.	Amount Cr.
Oct. 1	Goods A/c (Library)......Dr. To Jagrati Book Centre (Being Books bought from...)		3000	3000
Oct. 3	Goods A/c (Stationery)....Dr. To cash A/c (Being stationery bought against cash)		2000	2000
Oct. 4	Salary A/c................Dr. To Cash A/c (Being cash paid for salaries to N.T. Staff		25000	25000
Oct. 7	Bank A/c...................Dr. To cash A/c		50000	50000

Cash Book records all cash transactions. It is divided into two sides. One, on the left, known as debit side, is used for recording receipts and the other, on the right hand, known as credit side, is used for recording payments. A format of the Cash Book is given below:

Date	Vr. No.	L.F.	Receipts			Payments					
			Particulars	Amount		Date	Vr. No.	L.F.	Parti-cular	Amount	
				Cash	Bank					Cash	Bank

Note: 1. It would be ideal to have the Bank Column in the cash itself. When cheques or Drafts are received from U.G.C. or other sources, they should be shown in the receipt column of Bank and similarly payments made by cheques should be shown in the payment column of Bank. It will present a ready picture of Bank A/c without going through long compilation work.

2. When cash is collected on account of fees, etc., first it should be shown in the Cash Column of Receipts. And when it is transferred to Bank, it should be shown in the Bank Column of Receipts and Cash Column of Payments.

Sometimes for the sake of convenience cash books have columns for cash as well as bank transactions also. In such a case all the entries which involve cash and also bank are recorded in cash book and other entries are recorded in journals.

The debit side of entry shall be recorded on the debit side of cash book and credit entry, on the credit side. Since both entries are of the same amount the balance of cash is not affected.

Ledger

The book that contains the accounts of various income, expenditure, assets and liabilities is known as a ledger. Ledger may be regarded as Book of secondary entries. This is written from the books of prime entries, as Cash Book, Journal, etc. Actually the entries in all primary books affecting the same accounts are classified and grouped as under different account-heads in the ledger.

Format of ledger:

Date	Particulars	FOLIO	Dr. Amount		Cr. Amount		Balance	
			Rs.	P.	Rs.	P.	Rs.	P.

IV.
ACCOUNTS PROCEDURES AND PROFORMAS

Proper maintenance of accounts, and their close study to decide future strategy are very vital matters in the administration of a college.

Accounts have two sides:

A. Income
B. Expenditure

It is necessary that suitable proformas of various records, good guidelines and proper procedures to be followed must be developed. Here are some suggestions for consideration.

A. Income Side

1. Colleges have mainly fee income. Therefore, proper fee receipt should be evolved.
2. On an average one fee clerk should be able to collect fees of about 800 to 900 students. This should help in fixing the number of fee clerks.
3. Fee clerk must prepare Scholars, Registers — Class-wise and in an alphabetical order so that the serial may remain intact up to the time of sending examination forms, etc., to the University.

4. It is in the fitness of things that the income and expenditure of major funds are kept separately so that proper monitoring may be possible. Therefore, separate book of accounts must be opened for these funds and the Fee Receipts must have separate columns for them.
5. It will be advisable to have the following funds in separate accounts:

I. *Boys Funds Accounts*

1. Games Fund and Swimming Pool Fund Account.
2. Students Welfare Fund and Students Aid Fund Account.
3. Students Society Account, if any.

II. *Maintenance Fund Accounts*

1. Tuition Fees, D.A. Fees, Scholar Registration Fees, Fine Fees Account.
2. Science Fees and Lab Fees Account.
3. Development Fees Account.
4. Library Fees Account.
5. Hot and Cold Fees and Fan Fees Account.

III. *Miscellaneous Fund Accounts*

1. Incidental charges account.
2. Magazine fees and Identity Card Fee Account.
3. University Examinations Fees and University Enrolment fees account.
4. Urgent T.C. and C.C. fees account.

   The Format of this fees receipt is shown in Appendix A.

6. Thus approximately eleven Bank Accounts may have to be opened.
7. Every page of Fee Receipt Book can have receipts for 5-6 students. The grand total of all receipts of a page should be done, columnwise, at the end.

8. Fee clerk should consolidate the days collection on a separate register having the same columns as on fee receipt. One more column should be added, i.e., "Receipt Page No. with data". Suppose, one fee clerk charges fees from 60 students, in a day. The fees consolidation statement should show column-wise total of all ten pages. He should sign it and produce Fee Receipt Book alongwith this consolidated fee Registrar to Accountant/Cashier.
9. The Accountant/Cashier should check these two documents, receive the day's fees collection and sign the registers as a token of having checked them and received money. He must keep the original copy of the consolidated Fee Register and return the carbon copy along with the register to the fee clerk.
10. The fee clerk should also post student's ledger so that it may remain up to date.
11. Accountant/Cashier should send the fees thus realised to the Bank next morning without fail.
12. Accountant/Cashier should complete the Cash Books next day and get them signed by the Principal after showing the Bank receipts and also fee clerks' consolidated statements. He should maintain as may cash books as the number of Bank Accounts are.
13. If the college has other sources of income, its Bank Accounts, its receipt book, and its Cash-books should also be kept separately. It will be advisable to keep the following separate accounts:

    i) Rent account.
    ii) Donation account.
    iii) U.G.C. grants account.
    iv) State Govt. Grants account.

B. Expenditure Side

1. The various Incharges/Persons who have to make purchases, etc., must be informed of the Budget allocation in the month of April-May.
2. These Persons should also be informed about:

    i) The Impresst money which they can keep with them.

ii) The Rules of purchases and spending Imprest money.

N.B. : Draft procedure of purchase is shown in Appendix B and other Proformas are shown in Appendix C, D and E.

3. The Cash books must be written on the basis of actual expenditure.
4. A separate register should be prepared to show issue of cheques. This record should show cheque No., Date, Amount and name of the party. On the basis of monthly bank statement, in the last column of this register it should be recorded against each cheque that the payment was cleared on such and such date.
5. A separate advance register should be prepared showing the date of advance, the amount advanced, purpose of the advance and name of the person to whom advanced. As soon as the account of this advance is received, it should be recorded in the last column of this register.
   As a rule, the person receiving advance should submit the Account within a week of completion of the concerned work. Notice should be sent to the defaulters every month.
6. It is essential to get Bank statements, every month and reconcile them with the college records.

C. Some Important Documents

With a view to managing things in a more scientific way, the following documents should be used:

1. Every college employees should be given a Salary Account Book — Appendix 'F' (This is one sheet. There should be such 10 sheets in one book).
2. Every college employee should be given an Identity Card — Appendix 'G'.
3. Every college employee should be given a file in which following informations be provided:

   a) Leave Rules.
   b) Self-assessment Form to be submitted at the end of every year — vide Agra University Statutes.

c) Service Rules.
d) Copy of code of conduct alongwith college expectations.
e) Any other matter which is deemed important.

4. Every college must maintain separate files:

a) All Government orders concerning Financial Matters — Salary fixation, D.A., House Allowance, Pension, Gratuity, etc. Missing orders must be secured.
b) All Government orders — Non-Financial matters.
c) All University orders — separate files, category-wise.
d) U.P. Universities Act and copies of amendments.
e) Statute and ordinance and copies of amendments.
f) Other relevant papers.

V.
THE COLLEGE BUDGET

To prepare a college budget is one of the most important exercises and the Principal should take an active interest in getting it prepared and passed. The Statutes of some of Universities require that the Budget should be got prepared by the Principal and passed by the college management.

A Budget is for a 12-month period. The Government financial years are from April to March. So, normally, the college budgets are also for the period April to March. It may be remembered that the college academic session is from July to June. So it would have been best had the college financial year would have also been from July to June. But under the circumstance the budget should be from April to March but it should be broken into two:

a) April to June, i.e., 3 months. In this period the income from fee, etc., is almost negligible but the expenses are maximum.
b) July to March, i.e., 9 months.

Preparation of the college budget is almost a mathematical exercise which should be taken on the basis of previous years actuals and slight imagination.

The budget has two sides — Income and Expenditure.

Here are broad hints of how to prepare a Budget.

A. **Income Side**

For assessing the budgeted income for the current session, we need

a) Figures of past few years' admissions to various classes;
b) Figures of past few years of students who filled in the Examination Forms in different classes.
c) The fee schedule.

Experience tells that there is a fall-out of about 10 per cent students after taking admissions. The figures of past few years of admissions and those who filled in Examinations forms, or still better, those who appeared in the Examinations will give a clear indication of fallouts of a particular college. While calculating income, the fee income of these drop outs should be ignored. The income from fees of these fall out students be kept to meet emergencies or miscalculations.

Suppose the expected admissions, on the basis of past few years figures, in B.A. Part I are as below:

B.A. I : 500 students
The subject-wise break up is:

English Lit.	100
Hindi Lit.	250
English General	200
Hindi General	450
Economics	350
Geography	250
Psychology	150
Home Science	250
	2000, i.e., 500 students

We have not to calculate the income on the basis of 500 students admitted but say 10 per cent less — keeping a margin for drop-outs. So, the figures are:

	Admission	Dropout	Actual
English Lit.	100	10	90
Hindi Literature	250	25	225
English General	200	20	180
Hindi General	450	45	405
Economics	350	35	315
Geography	250	25	225
Psychology	150	15	135
Home Science	250	25	225
	2000	200	1800

i.e., 450 students.

On the basis of fee schedule the income of different fee heads for different classes can be calculated as below:

Heads	Fee (Rs.)	No. of Students (If 500 admitted)	Annual income (In Rs.)
1. Prospectus fee	5	450	2250.00
2. Registration fee	1	450	450.00
3. Admission fee	3	450	1350.00
4. Development fee	20 p.a.	450	9000.00
5. Student Welfare fee	18 p.a.	450	8100.00
6. Poor boys fee	12 p.a.	450	5400.00
7. College Magazine fee	10 p.a.	450	4500.00
8. Fan fee	5 p.a.	450	2250.00
9. Hot and cold fee	6 p.a.	450	2700.00
10. Library fee	12 p.a.	450	5400.00
11. Games fee	10 p.a	450	4500.00
12. Annual function fee	1 p.a.	450	450.00
13. D.A. fees	25 p.a.	450	11250.00
14. Tuition fee	132 p.a.	450	59400.00
15. Practical subject fee	@ 2 per subject p.m.		
a) Geography	24 p.a.	225	5400.00
b) Psychology	24 p.a.	135	3240.00
c) Home Science	24 p.a.	225	5400.00

As per Government rules in U.P. the entire fee income is not to be kept by the college. Some fees are to be kept 100 per cent, somc

25 per cent, some 20 per cent and so on. Hence, out of these expected income figures, government share is to be deducted.

For example, 80 per cent tuition fees in case of students of Arts Faculty is to be surrendered to the Government. So, the college share of income comes as below:

Tuition Fees Rs. 59,400 p.a.
80% of Rs. 59,400 = Rs. 47,520
i.e. Rs. 11,880 college share

In this way, we can calculate the total expected income of the college for the full year.

The normal practice is to give figures in two sets — Estimated and Actuals. The figures of past few years are given so as to give an idea of how much the exercise was correct or how much it went wrong. If it went wrong then the Principal should know the factors which were responsible for it. These factors should be taken into consideration while calculating income of the current year.

The presentation will be something like this:

Income

Heading on 450 students	1984-85 Est. Rs.	Act.	1985-86 Est. Rs.	Act. Rs.	1986-87 Est. Rs.	Act	1987-88 Est.	Remarks
1. Prospectus	2250	2500	2250	2400	2250	2350	2200	These figs. show that number of admission is falling. So income will fall corrective steps be taken.
2. Tuition fee	11880	13000	11880	12500	11880	12000	12500	These figures show that drop-out is increasing.

It will be ideal if the Fees Receipts Forms arrange fees under broad heading such as:

1. *Maintenance Funds* — Tuition fees, D.A. Fees, Scholar Register Fees, Lab Fees, Library Fees, Hot and Cold Fees etc.
2. *Students Fund* — Games Fund, Students Aid Fund, Students' Union Fund.
3. *Other Funds* — Magazine Fees, Identity Card Fees, T.C. & C.C. fees, Enrolment Fees, Examination Fees etc.

N.B. — See Appendix A.

The time for charging fees is an important decision. Following ideas are worth consideration:

i) If there are more than one college in the town, students will like to study in that college which is giving better facilities and they will seek admission there. For example, if at the time of admission, one college is charging Rs. 200 and another college Rs. 150 the natural tendency for the students will be to go to more beneficial college. In such a situation:

   a) All the colleges of a town should make a common strategy. Normally this does not work due to obvious reasons.
   b) Evaluate, from students' point of view, the relative importance of your college and accordingly decide which annual fees are to be charged at the time of admission and how much of it — 100 per cent, or 50 per cent or 25 per cent.
   c) While taking this decision, let us not forget that there will be less revenue on account of dropouts. And so efforts should be to minimise this loss.

ii) Efforts should be made to make students pay fees every month. This will ensure minimum loss of income to the college under various heads. In real life, this appears to be difficult as it is not easy to strike off names and charge re-admission fees. Moreover, the number of fee clerks may be insufficient. However, efforts should be made for it. A common policy for all the affiliated colleges will be useful.

iii) Insistence should be not to allow any student to fill in the Examination Form till he clears the dues up to date. If possible he must pay even for next one or two months.

iv) It should be ensured that no student is allowed to appear in practical Examination till he clears the dues for the whole session. It will stagger the work load on Accounts Office and ensure income to the college for making rush payments.

v) The college may receive grants/subsidies from U.G.C./ Central Govt./Directorate, etc. The amount thus received must be spent on the item for which it has been received. This will help in balancing the budget by reducing the allocation from maintenance fees.

B. Expenditure Side

While budgeting expenditure, several things should be kept in mind:

i) The relative importances of expenditure : In these days of rising price and income remaining almost constant, one has to cut-down expenses. So, a beginning should be made from the least important items.

ii) The rate of increase in prices: The Index number will give this idea. The budgeted amounts should be increased, keeping in mind the increase in the prices of those items.

iii) The past few years' actual expenditures will give an indication.

iv) Efforts should be made that the income for a particular purpose and the expenditure on it should be balanced. The transfer of income from one item to the other should be avoided and should be done only when essential. For example, the practical fees Income of Arts subjects is substantial. It should not be spent on these subjects. It will be profitable to divert it to expenditure on practicals of Science subjects where the fee income is normally insufficient.

v) Efforts should be made to find out how expenditure can be reduced. For example, a G.O. of the electricity Deptt. of U.P. says that if all electric connections are clubbed and one single point delivery is taken then the additional rebate will be given. Hospitals and educational institutions can benefit by it.

vi) Provisions should be made for certain amounts for welfare activities of students, teachers and non-teachers. This will generate a feeling of belonging to the college. For example, uniforms should be provided to Class IV employees. It will give a better look, generate a sense of unity and discipline and may command loyalty.

vii) A marginal surplus budget should always be had as it, along with extra income from dropouts, will act as a cushion for unforeseen expenses.

viii) While allotting money to various items, a basis may be thought out. For example, in matters of Deptt. upkeep, the basis can be per student. Similarly, in matters of Library allotment, subject-wise, two bases can be taken together — the one per student and the other cost of books of the subject. For example, Hindi books are cheaper than books in English. So, per capita basis for Hindi should be lower than that of English (for details see Chapter on Library).

The Expenditure side of the Budget should be in the following form:

Sl. No.	Item	Expenditure							
		1988-89		1989-90		1990-91		1991-92	
		Est. Rs.	Act.	Est. Rs.	Act.	Est. Rs.	Act.	Est. Rs.	
1.	Maintenance of Deptt.								
	a) Physics	5000	5500	5000	6000	5000	6250	7000	When prices are rising, you should allot realistic amount.
	b) Chemistry	7000	8000	7000	9000	7000	9500	10000	
	c) Geography	1000	600	1000	650	1000	750	800	
	d) Psychology	1000	400	1000	450	1000	500	550	
2.	Hot & Cold	2000	2100	2000	2500	2000	3000	4000	Electricity consumption will increase as Electricity rates are going up and prices of bulbs, etc., are also rising. Moreover, with passage of time consumption also increases.

(*Contd.*)

Sl. No.	Item	1988-89 Est. Rs.	1988-89 Act. Rs.	1989-90 Est. Rs.	1989-90 Act. Rs.	1990-91 Est. Rs.	1990-91 Act. Rs.	1991-92 Est. Rs.	
		Expenditure							
3.	Advertise-ment	2000	2500	2000	2000	2000	1500	1000	Since in U.P. vacancies are to be filled in by Higher Education Service Commission, one can economise and instead of advertising the post, help may be taken from Employment Exchange for class IV posts and rules of promotion be used for class III posts.

C. Summing Up

When we put income and expenditure sides together, the full Budget proposals are prepared.

Two different Budgets, one of maintenance and another of Students' Fund, should be prepared.

The budget of maintenance only, has to be passed by the Management.

To prepare budget is the one thing and to keep a Financial control, is another. How to do it is important.

VI.
FINANCIAL CONTROL

For a better control and accounting the following suggestions are worth consideration:

1. If possible, change to Double Entry System.
2. Check the cash book daily and sign it.
3. Ensure that the day's net cash collections are sent to Bank either the same day or early the next day and check daily deposits with Bank receipts. This would serve as a safeguard against any possible misappropriations.
4. Maintain a Bank Register so that you can keep a track of various credits and debits in the Bank, and can easily prepare a reconciliation of Bank balance with your cash book or bank book balance. A Format of Bank Register is given in Appendix H.

   It should be ensured that the Bank reconciliation is prepared regularly at monthly intervals.
5. It has been observed by me during the checking of college accounts that many times cheques are issued without ascertaining the balance in the account and as a consequence the cheques are dishonoured creating difficulty for the payees and affecting the credibility of the college. It is therefore, suggested that before issuing a cheque it should be ensured that there is sufficient balance in the bank. This could be done by keeping a track of the debits and credits in the bank and noting the same in the Bank Register. This also makes the maintenance of Bank Register a necessity.
6. Insist on maintaining an advance register in which all advances given should be entered along with the name of the person taking advance, date of taking advance, purpose of advance and name of authority who sanctioned the advance. Further, as soon as the person submits account of the advance, the date and particulars of adjustment should be mentioned therein. From the register a list of advances outstanding at the end of each month be prepared and notices be given to all with whom advances are outstanding for long.

   It is observed that generally people are prompt in taking advance but are slack in submitting adjustments. This register would assist in knowing the amount of advances and from whom it is recoverable and would consequently assist in early settlement/adjustment. The maintenance of such a register is very essential in case of single entry accounts such as schools, colleges, etc.
7. It is a common experience that Departments have a tendency

of incurring expenses in excess of amounts allotted to them in the budget, or the budgeted limits are exhausted even though certain important items of expenses are still to be incurred. These either lead to an excess expenditure thereby upsetting the budget allocations or if there is a paucity of funds, important expenses, projects have to be deferred. This happens because no track is generally kept of the amount of expenditure made up to a particular date and the extent of unavailed limit remaining.

In order to avoid this, it is essential that before sanctioning any expenditure the sanctioning authority should ensure that the expenditure to be incurred shall be within the overall limit and that this expenditure would not affect expenditure on any other important item yet to be incurred.

For this it is suggested that a ledger or register be maintained giving the particulars of the total sanctioned budgeted amount and the important items of expenditure which are necessarily to be incurred out of the sanctioned amount. Besides, it should also give the total amount of expenditure already incurred, the total of bills pending and the total of orders not yet executed. This would help in exercising proper control.

8. A periodical trial balance should be prepared from the books of accounts to make sure that the accounts have been maintained correctly. This will help in detecting and correcting mistakes before it is too late.
9. It is also advisable to maintain stock register of goods purchased. This would help in keeping a control over the property of the college. In case of schools or colleges it would be better to maintain such a register department-wise or on some other basis where the responsibility for maintenance and control can be fixed. The stock register should give the name of item, quantity, value and its location. The department needs or other authorised persons should periodically verify physically the items and make a mention of this fact in the register.
10. Normally the motive of the college is not to earn profit. But even then for better control, a periodical income and expenditure account should be prepared. This would help in exercising a better control over income and expenditure.
11. It is essential that the audit objections raised by Government

Auditors or other Auditors, if any, should be promptly looked into and got rectified. Delay or slackness in the matter may pose problems for the institution, *e.g.,* the Director of Higher Education or Government may stop or cancel a particular grant or delay its release.

12. It has been observed that at times no proper accounts are maintained for the special grants received from various agencies or the expenditure incurred is not exactly as per the terms of sanction. This is a serious lapse and the authority giving the grant may subsequently cancel the grant.

APPENDIX A

FORMAT OF FEE RECEIPT

Book No. Receipt No.

Name

Class Roll No./Subj. Date	Maintenance Fund												
	S. Registration	Admission	Tuition fee	D.A.	Science	Laboratories	Fines	Total	Development	Library	Hot and Cold	Fans	Total
1	2	3	4	5	6	7	8	9	10	11	12	13	14

(*Contd.*)

(*Contd.*)

Name	Boys Funds						Misc. Funds								
Class Roll No./ Subj. Date	Games	Swim-ming	Stu-dents Wel-fare	Stu-dents Aid	Stu-dents So-ciety	Total	Inci-dental	Maga-zine	Id-entity card	Univ. Exam.	Univ. Enrol-ment	Urgent T.C., C.C.	Others	Total	
1	15	16	17	18	19	20	21	22	23	24	25	26	27	28	
															Total
															Total B/F
															Total C.O.

Date

Signature of Fee Clerk
Name of College

APPENDIX B

NOTICE

PROCEDURE OF PURCHASE
(1992-93)

The College has finalised the following procedure for purchases which will come into force immediately:

1. That the quotations will be invited and purchases will be made from the parties who quote lowest net prices. The following parties are already registered with the college and they have agreed to give the commission mentioned against their name with a provision that the supplies will be executed within a reasonable time:

(a) M/s 12%
(b) M/s 10%
(c) M/s

Department should invite quotations from other parties also — local and outside.

2. Quotation should be called in writing, preferably from those parties who are the producers/sellers/agents of items to be purchased. While inviting quotations full specification of the item to be purchased be given.

3. It may be ensured that parties who are not registered in Sales Tax do not charge S.T.

4. The Department will invite quotations in a sealed cover addressed to Incharge of the Department of .... College, ... Parties should be advised to write "Quotation for .... Department" at the top of the sealed envelop. The concerned Incharge should sign these envelops and put the date of receipt of quotation. These quotations will be opened by the Principal (In the presence of the Incharge of the Department) on the last date of quotations and sign at the top.

5. In case a quotation is received late from a standard concern it

can be considered only after taking special permission in writing from the Principal. No quotations are needed if the purchase is below Rs. 100 but if a single item is purchased for more than Rs. 20 the quotations are required.

N.B.: No quotations are required for placing an order of the Library books.

6. If three quotations could not be secured, or cannot be secured, the reason should be clearly mentioned by the Incharge in his remarks column (comparative chart).

7. The Incharge, will prepare a comparative chart of the quotations received and will make positive recommendations regarding purchases in the prescribed proforma (Appendix C) available in the department. Items should be marked with red ink indicating the firm from which it will be purchased. If an item is to be purchased on higher rate, the reasons of deviation be clearly mentioned.

8. The comparative chart along with the quotations duly opened will be sent within 3 days to the office of the Principal of the receipt of quotations by the department concerned.

9. The department must send the requisition to the office after entering them in a register which should show the amount allotted to the Department and the amount of the orders already placed. In no case the departments should exceed the allocations.

10. The O.S./Bursar will scrutinise these quotations and give his recommendations mainly from the audit point of view. In this regard no objection will be entertained at the stage of passing the bill if it is in conformity with the quotations approved and order placed by the college.

11. The O.S./Bursar will send all requisitions collected in the day, to the Principal who will normally clear them within two days. If the college Secretary has to finally approve the order, the papers will be sent to the college Secretary.

12. The department will be informed of the orders of the Principal/Secretary by the O.S./Bursar. The Department will thereupon prepare the order in four copies and get the signatures of the Principal. The original copy will be sent to the supplier. The second copy will be enclosed with the Bill while sending it for payment to the Bursar. Form of the order is Appendix D.

13. The order number should carry the name of the Department such as "Bot/No................./87-88 dated.............."

14. The supplier should invariably be directed to send the bill in

triplicate to the Department concerned C/o.. College.

15. The Department will check up the goods and will send the original copy of the bill alongwith all connected papers to O.S./Bursar within three days of the receipt of goods on a Bill-cum-Stock Book.

16. The Bursar/O.S. will issue a receipt of the bill book to the Department immediately. The O.S./Bursar will scrutinise the documents and put up the entire papers before the Principal (and later College Secretary) for necessary orders. The bill book in every case will be returned to the Department within 2 days of the receipt. If the O.S./Bursar has any objections, he will reduce them to writing on a separate paper (not on the Bill) and return them to the Department after Principal's counter signatures within 2 days. A copy of these objections will be preserved by the O.S./Bursar for future use.

17. The O.S./Bursar will pass on these passed bills alongwith concerned papers to Accountant who will prepare the cheques within next 3 days and will enter them in a register. The cheques will normally be crossed and marked 'Account payee'.

18. The Accountant will send the cheques daily except Monday and Tuesday) alongwith the connected papers and register to the Principal/College Secretary in the evening and the Treasurer the next morning (if needed) for signature who will sign cheques and pass orders for payment. The cheques will be accompanied by the pay order form duly filled in (Appendix E).

19. The cheques duly signed will be handed over to the despatch clerk who sill despatch them by post within 2 days under Certificate of Posting (local including departments by personal delivery).

20. The O.S./Bursar will himself prepare a register department-wise and party-wise (a sort of ledger in which the date of placement of order, the date of receipt of bills and the date of despatch of cheques will be entered along with the amount paid. This is useful to reconcile Bank statement.

Thus the payment should be sent to the party normally within 15 days of the receipt of bill. If the payment is delayed unnecessarily by anyone, it will be his personal responsibility and the college shall be free to take action against the person concerned.

21. To rationalize purchases the Department should finish department purchases by the middle of February so that no bill may remain pending for payment after 15th of March.

22. The departmental imprest accounts should be submitted after 50% of the expenditure is incurred so that by the time the recoupment is made to Incharge concerned the departmental work may not be held up for want of funds.

23. The imprest account will also be paid in the same way as other bills are paid, hence the recoupment will take maximum a week's time.

24. (a) No individual voucher of Imprest purchase should be of more than Rs. 20.00.

(b) No quotation will be required for making purchases out of imprest money for petty items.

(c) Sanction is invariably necessary for making purchase from imprest money, if the amount involved is of more than Rs. 20.

(d) The responsibility for the proper utilisation of imprest will be of the Incharge of department and not only of the person supposed to do it as Incharge imprest.

(e) The Imprest money of the various departments for the session .... will be as below:

(i) Physics –	Rs. ______
(ii) Botany and Botanical Garden –	Rs. ______
(iii) Zoology –	Rs. ______
(iv) Geology –	Rs. ______
(v) Chemistry –	Rs. ______
(vi) Geography –	Rs. ______
(vii) Drawing –	Rs. ______
(viii) Mil.St. –	Rs. ______
(ix) Psychology –	Rs. ______
(x) Electricity –	Rs. ______
(xi) Gardens –	Rs. ______
(xii) Furniture –	Rs. ______
(xiii) Building –	Rs. ______

The persons going out on college work must obtain prior permission from the Principal. The T.A. Bills should be submitted on the printed form available with the Accountant as per college T.A. & D.A. Rules.

The Accountant will maintain a separate register for T.A. Bills in which all the necessary entries will be made.

25. Since the Government and College audit has become more

strict, it is essential that the dates of quotations, requisitions, sanctions, orders and cash memos should be in a proper order. It is also essential that proper cash memos should be submitted as saving of taxes, etc., does not prove helpful from the point of economy but sometimes puts the college in an odd position when it becomes necessary to locate a supplier to authenticate the expenditure involved.

26. Please write to the parties, at the time of placing order that 'D' form will not be submitted.

27. Cash payment can be made to those parties who allow cash discount on the purchases. In such payments, 90% will be released after receipt of goods in the department and balance 10% after the clearance of the bill by the Office. This discount should be more than 2%. However, all the payments should be made within 10 days. In case the payment is not made within 10 days the persons responsible for the delays will be liable for action.

PRINCIPAL

APPENDIX C

.... COLLEGE

Department of ....
Amount allotted ....

Amount spent ....
Amount for which
Sanction obtained ....

Comparative Statement of Quotations and Requisition for Purchase

Amount of present
Requisition ....

Sl. No.	Name & Specifications of Articles		Names of Firms along with their Quotations				Quantity in hand	Purchased in last session	Quantity required	Amount sanction required	Firm from which it is to be purchased (S. No.)	Remarks
	Name	Specification										
1	2	3	4	5	6	7	8	9	10	11	12	13

I/c of the Department

Principal

Chairman
Purchase Committee/Secretary

APPENDIX D

ORDER FORM

Original

..............................COLLEGE

Order No. __________ Deptt. of _______ Dated _____

To
M/s. ____

____

With reference to your quotation/letter No. .... Dated .... you are requested to supply the undermentioned goods to the Deptt. concerned personally/by passenger train/goods train/post parcel/motor transport and forward the R.R./G.R./ direct through S.B.I. College Br./V.P.P.

Sl.No.	Particulars	Quantity required	Rate		Value	
					Rs.	P.
		Total cost				

General Conditions

(1) The material is subject to the approval by the Head of the department.
(2) The supply be made within .... days from the receipt of this order.
(3) Bills should be submitted in duplicate/triplicate.
(4) College will not issue Form 'D' hence the S.T. be charged accordingly.

Any other conditions:

Signature of the Head of the Deptt.

Seal & Signature of the Principal

APPENDIX E

..............................COLLEGE

Vr. No.......................
Dated ....

Debit		Head		
Amount to be paid to:			Rs.	P.
Amount (in words) Rupees......................................		Total Rs.		

Credit		Head		
Details:				
Amount (in words) Rupees......................................		Total Rs.		
1. Net payment Rupees 2. Amount to be recovered (if any)				

Prepared by **Accountant** **O.S./Bursar** **Principal** **Secretary**

The Cheque No. .... Dated .... of Rs. ....

of ....Bank has been prepared by me.

I have signed this cheque. Acctt. to pay

ACCOUNTANT

PRINCIPAL/SECRETARY

SALARY ACCOUNT BOOK

Salary Statement for the Year 19——19——

	Mar	Apr	May	Jun	July	Aug	Sep	Oct	Nov	Dec	Jan	Feb	Arrears	Total
Basic pay														
Personal pay														
D.A.														
% D.A.														
A.D.A.														
H.R.A.														
Interim relief														
Gross pay														
P.F. own Contr.														
G.P.F.														
Refd. of P.F. loan														
Arrears in PF/GPF														
Income Tax														
Group Ins.														
L.I.C. Prem.														
Credit Society loan														
Revenue Stamp														
Other deduction														
Net. Pay														
Management Contr.														

APPENDIX G

Photo of
Employee

IDENTITY CARD

NAME ....

NAME OF FATHER/HUSBAND ....

DESIGNATION ....

DEPARTMENT ....

DATE OF BIRTH ....

APPROVAL LETTER'S NO ....

S.B. A/c No. .... BANK ....

P.F. A/c No. ....BANK ....

RESIDENTIAL ADDRESS ....

....

PHONE No. ....

Whether Covered under Insurance
Scheme, if so, give details

Policy No.	Premium	Sum assured	Date of Maturity

NOMINATION

Priority	Name of Nominee	Age with Date of Birth	Relation

Signature or thumb
Impression of Nominee

Signature of employee

Note: It is in accordance with the nomination papers filed by me with regard to —

1. Provident Fund
2. Group/Insurance
3. Cooperative Society
4.

APPENDIX H

BANK RECONCILIATION STATEMENT

When money is deposited in the bank, the concern enters it on the debit side of bank account maintained by it and bank also enters it on the credit side of the concern's account maintained by the bank. So, it can be said that when amount or cheque is deposited in bank the concern debit the bank account and bank credits the concern account. Hence, the debit balance of bank account in the books of concern should be equal to the credit balance of concern's account in the books of bank.

Conversely, when money is withdrawn or cheque is issued bank debits the concern's account in its books and at the same time concern credits the bank account in its books. Therefore, the debit balance of concern's account in the books of banks should be equal to the credit balance of the bank account in the books of concern.

But it is not usually so. Generally a difference is found in the books of the concern and the books of the bank. This difference may be due to many reasons. Unless these reasons are known, the books of account maintained by the concern cannot be treated to be correct. S. me times it may happen that some amount has been misappropriated by the cashier which can be detected only by comparing each and every entry in the books of concern and that of the banks.

Periodically, bank supplies a copy of the concern's account to the concern for the information, this is called the pass book or the bank statement. All entries in the debit side of bank account in the book of concern are found in the credit side of the bank statement and similarly all entries in the credit side in bank account in the book of concern are found in the debit side of the bank Statement. All these entries are compared and cross tallied and the entries remaining which can be detected and the reason for their remaining untick are detected. The various causes of difference in the books of concern and that of bank may be summarised as below:

(1) *Cheques deposited but not collected* — When cheques are deposited in the books of concern bank, account is immediately debited but in the books of bank 'the concern's account is not credited until they are actually collected by the bank. It is quite usual

that some of the cheques deposited by the concern may remain uncollected at the date on which the two account are compared. These can be found in the debit of the bank account in the books of concern remaining untick. To equalize the two balances, the concern should credit the amount of these cheques to reach at a situation before depositing the cheque. So this amount should be deducted from debit balance or added to the credit balance in the books of the concern.

(2) *Cheques issued but not presented* — When cheques are issued, the concern credits that bank account in its books, but in the books of bank entry for payment can be made only when cheque is presented for payment and actually paid by the bank. At the time of comparison it is quite possible that some cheques are issued by the concern but they are not presented before the bank. These can be found in the credit side of ledger in bank account.

(3) *Bank Charges* — Bank render many services to its clients and for that it lavies some charges, i.e. locker rent, cheque collection charges, incidental charges, etc. For it bank makes the entry immediately by debiting the client's account but the corresponding entry is not found in the concern's books. These can be found in debit side of bank statement remaining untick.

Taking bank overdraft as per ledger, the reconciliation statement will be as follows:

Bank Reconciliation Statement with. . . . . .Bank as on. . . . .

Overdraft as per cash book — Rs.

Add:

i) Cheques sent for collection but not collected:
ii) Cheques sent for collection but dishonoured
iii) Bank charges by bank

Less:

i) Cheques issued but not presented for payment
ii) Cheque issued but dishonoured by bank
iii) Amount directly deposited by customers

Balance as per bank statement Dr.

Procedure of Reconciling the Bank Account

After all the entries in the ledger are compared with the similar entries in the bank statement, we can ascertain the untick entries. If there are untick entries in the debit side of bank account, i.e. cheques sent for collection but not collected, these entries should be deleted i.e. we should reduce the debit balances, or in case of a credit balance in ledger, the same should be added to the credit balance.

Similarly, if there are untick entries in the credit side, i.e. cheques issued but not presented for payment, these should be deleted by reducing the credit balance or by adding to the debit balance. So that the balances of concern and the bank become equal.

If there are some untick entries in the debit side of bank statement i.e. bank charges, *etc.*, a credit entry should exist in the books of concern, to take its effect, the amount should be added to the credit balance or in case of debit balance in the books, the same should be deducted from debit balance.

On the other hand if some untick entries in the credit side of bank statement i.e. direct payments by parties, the same should be debited to the Bank account of the concern, to take its effect, the amount should either be added to the debit balance or deducted from the credit balance.

By adding and deducting the amounts as mentioned above, the balance of ledger account must become equal to the balance as shown by the bank statement.

(4) *Cheque dishonoured* — Sometimes it may happen that cheque issued by the concern are dishonoured by bank due to some causes of which no intimation is received by the concern, so these items shall remain untick in credit side of bank account in the ledger.

(5) *Direct Payment* — Some customers deposit money directly into the account in the bank, the corresponding entry of which may not appear in the cash book due to delay in necessary instructions by the customers. Such entries can be found in credit side of bank statement.

(6) *Errors* — Besides this, there could be difference due to errors in recording the transactions by any of the two parties. It may be either a totaling difference of ledger or bank statement or an amount under or over written or any amount completely omitted in either of the books.

(7) *How the rectify the difference* — In order to rectify the dif-

ference a statement called bank reconciliation statement is prepared. The form of the bank reconciliation statement is given below:

Bank reconciliation statement with . . . . .Bank as on. . . . . .19. . . . . .

Balance as per ledger (Dr.) Rs.

Add:

i) Cheques issued but not presented for payment
ii) Cheques issued but dishonoured by bank
iii) Amount directly deposited by customers
iv) Interest credited by bank

Less:

i) Cheques issued for collection but not collected
ii) Cheques issued for collection but dishonoured
iii) Bank charges debited by bank

Balance as per bank Statement (Cr.)

5

COLLEGE BUILDINGS

College building is an essential infrastructural of education. The building creates a visible impact. If the building is well maintained and presents a majestic look, immediately the onlooker gathers an impression that the institution is good. Conversely, if the building is not well maintained and not well planned, it creates a poor impression. It must be remembered that in modern times glitter is more important. Besides this visible impact, it also has same co-relation with the efficiency of teaching. If for example, class-rooms are small in size, it will be difficult to accommodate the students of a section properly. And when a student is unable to sit properly, neither he can concentrate well, nor can the teacher feel at ease. There is bound to be indiscipline. The same is true of laboratories, library, administrative block, etc. Similarly, if they are poorly ventilated, dark and dingy there cannot be ease either in teaching or reading.

A college building includes, besides class-rooms, laboratories, etc., roads, drains, toilets, electric installations and water supply. It includes gardens and lawns also.

The Principal of a college should know the following things about a college building:

1. How to maintain and improve the existing buildings and also make their optimal use.
2. How to plan new buildings — location and design on the basis of use.

It is obvious that the building's maintenance and design and construction of new building is a technical job and a Principal ordinarily is not expected to be an expert in these matters. He must hire the services of experts of it. But he must have sufficient insight to tell the experts his problems, requirements and thinking about future development.

As per statutory provisions and also convention, the maintenance of old building and construction of new buildings is the sole responsibility of the college management. So, a understanding and active cooperation between the Principal and the college Secretary is essential. Normally, it is lacking.

I.
OLD BUILDINGS

There are two aspects concerning old buildings:

1. Maintenance
2. Optimal and scientific use

It will be advisable to have some broad hints about the two here.

Repairs and Maintenance

It has been observed that the buildings of colleges are not properly maintained and as a result their life span is considerably reduced. The reason for poor maintenance may be:

(i) *Financial Constraints*

Normally a college has no budget provision for annual repairs and the government funding agencies also do not give grants for this purpose.

The college management should make some recurring budget provision either through some form of fees charged from students or from their own internal resources to make funds available for repair work.

(ii) *Manpower*

Most of the colleges resort to engaging labour either privately or through contract for short period mostly in summer vacations. This generally comes out to be expensive and the work is also of not good quality because of lack of supervision. To manage this activity better, a building maintenance section headed by a technical person can be created. This will function under the direct supervision of the Principal. Activities like building repairs, electrical and mechanical repairs, plumbing, gardening, conservancy, etc., can be put under this section. The following sectional organization may be effective (Fig. 5.1):

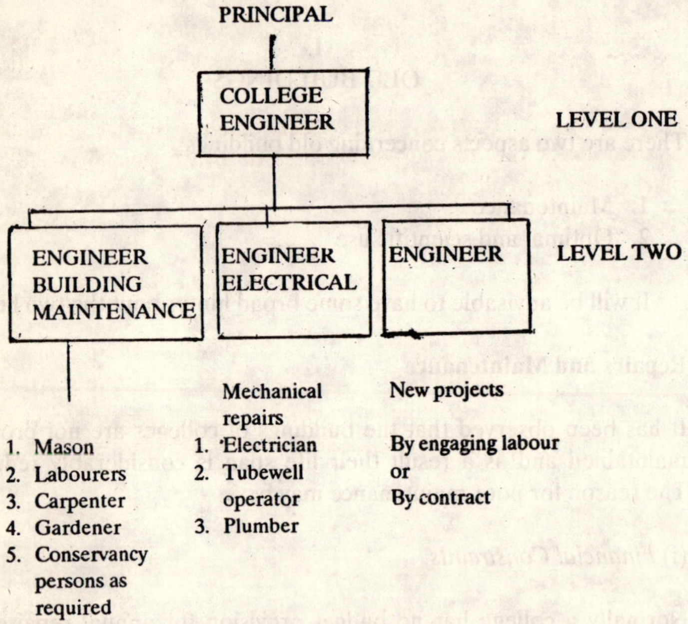

FIG. 5.1: College Maintenance Organisation

The college should have budget provision for this. For small size colleges, persons at level one can be omitted and only or two technical persons at level two may supervise the workers. It will be a good idea to appoint retired technical hands on part time basis and/or have an architect and structural engineer as consultant.

Role of College Engineer

The person shall be of the rank of an Assistant Engineer with long experience of building work. He will be responsible for the over all maintenance of buildings, roads, electrical and mechanical installation, execution of new construction, maintenance of garden, sports fields, etc. He will also assist the Principal in applying for and obtaining financial grants, obtaining approval of works from local authority, purchase of materials, etc.

Role of Engineer in Building Maintenance

The person shall be of the rank of Junior Engineer with sufficient experience. He shall work under the direction and to the satisfaction of college engineer. He will supervise the work of mason, carpenter, gardener and conservancy staff working under him. He should be responsible for the up-keep of building furniture, garden, roads, etc. Jointly with the college engineer he has to prepare scheme for the annual maintenance works to be taken up with the funds allotted.

Engineer (Electrical/Mechanical)

The person shall be of the rank of a Junior Engineer with sufficient experience. He will work under the direction and to the satisfaction of college engineer. He will be responsible for the maintenance of all electrical and mechanical installation in the college as well as maintenance of water and sewer line.

(iii) *Cleanliness*

Normally the college building is not kept neat and clean. One can see dirt all around. Cobwebs, wall writing, posters, marks of spirit, etc., mark the walls and floors. Heaps of refuge are found scattered here and there. Roads and foot-paths have dirt, pits, filth and over grown grass. The toilets and bath-rooms are stinking. Taps are non-functional. All this gives a very shabby appearance. It is essential that the sweepers, gardeners, watermen and other class four employees are allotted areas and rooms. It should be their duty to keep the premises neat and clean and dust the students' furniture each day before the college starts. One hour duty will be sufficient. There is very little work when teaching work remains suspended but the class III and IV staff is on duty. Such day should be utilised for a thorough cleaning of the walls, ceiling and ventilators, etc., with brushes of soft grooms. *Daftri* must be asked to supervise and report lapses. A teacher should be made over-all incharge. The Principal himself should keep a watchful eye. The old principle of reward and punishment should be effectively employed.

(iv) *Plaster*

In old buildings, plaster peels out. It exposes the brick to sun and rain and thereby adversely effect the life of the building, besides presenting a shabby look. It is necessary that such walls should be plastered at the earliest possible opportunity.

It has been observed that the maximum damage to plaster is done up to the plinth area. The dampness also causes damage. It will be advisable to get such areas plastered with *badarpur* sand instead of river sand. If necessary, damp proof powder may be mixed in the mortar and the plaster should be thoroughly rubbed and smoothened. The cause of dampness should be removed.

(v) *White-washing*

It must be a regular practice to get the building white-washed at regular intervals. If the entire building cannot be white-washed at a time, it must be divided in groups and each part should be got white-washed in a cyclic order.

(vi) *Sewage System*

Most of the college buildings do not have a proper drainage system – neither open no underground. It is not a desirable thing. On priority basis, the drains should be got constructed so that the water — rain or dirty water — does not seep around buildings. It will be advisable to have an underground sewage system.

(vii) *Roofs and Rain Water*

It has been noticed that in the old buildings either the roofs were not made on the slab or they have become useless with passage of time. So, it will be desirable to get them rebuilt. It will enhance the life of the building.

Proper drains for rain water should also be provided. Instead of open outlets, it will be desirable to provide plastic pipes.

(viii) *Anti-Termite Treatment*

Sub-terranean termites are responsible for most of the termite damage in buildings. Typically, they form nests on colonies underground in the soil near ground level in a stump or other suitable piece of timber in a conical or dome shaped mound. The termite find access to the super-structure of the building either through the timber buried in the ground or by means of mud shelter tubes constructed over unprotected foundations.

Termite control in existing as well as new building structure is very important, as the damage likely to be caused by the termites to wooden members of buildings and other articles like furniture, fittings, stationery, etc., is considerable. Anti-termite treatment can be either (1) During the time of construction, i.e., pre-constructional chemical treatment or (2) After the building has been constructed, i.e., treatment for existing building.

Prevention of the termite from reaching the super-structure of the building and its contents can be achieved by creating a chemical barrier between the ground, from where the termites come and other contents of the building which may form food for the termites. This is achieved by treating the soil beneath the building and around the foundation with a suitable insecticide.

Materials : Any one of the following chemicals (as specified) in water emulsion shall be used:

	Concentration (per cent)
Dieldrin Emulsifiable concentrates (IS: 1054)	0.5
Aldrin emulsifiable concentrates (IS: 1307)	0.5
Heptachlor emulsifiable concentrates	0.5
Chlordane emulsifiable concentrates	1.0

Chemicals are available in concentrated form in the market and concentration is indicated on the sealed containers. To achieve the percentage of concentration specified above, chemical should be diluted with water in required quantity before it is used. Graduated containers shall be used for dilution of chemical with water in required proportion to achieve the desired percentage of concentration.

Example: To dilute chemical of 30 per cent concentration add 59 parts of water to one part of chemical to achieve 0.5 per cent concentration.

Chemicals shall be brought to site of work in sealed original containers. The material shall be brought in, at a time, in adequate quantity to suffice for the whole or at least a fort-night's work. The material shall be kept in the joint custody of the contractor and the Engineer-in-charge. The empties shall not be removed from the site of work, till the relevant item of work has been completed and permission obtained from the Engineer-in-charge.

How to Treat?

Once the termite have an ingress into the building, they keep on multiplying and destroy the wooden and cellulosic materials, and as such it becomes essential to take measures for protection against termites. Anti-termite measures described below are necessary for the eradication and control of termites in existing buildings. To facilitate proper penetrations of chemical into the surface to be treated, hand operated pressure pump shall be used. To have proper check for uniform penetration of chemical, graduated containers shall be used. Proper check should be kept that the specified quantity of chemical is used for the required area during the operation.

Treatment along Outside of Foundations

The soil in contact with the foundation along the external perimeter of the building shall be treated with chemical emulsion at the rate of 15 litre/m^2 of vertical surface of the sub-structure for each side. To facilitate this treatment, trenches shall be excavated equal to the width of a shovel exposing the foundation wall surfaces upto a depth of 500 mm (20") and holes 150 mm (6") apart made with an iron rod close to the wall face, shall be extended from the bottom of the trench to the top of the footing of the foundation or up to a depth of at least 500 mm (20"). Half the total quantity of chemical emulsion shall be poured into these holes and the rest sprayed on the back fill earth as it is required on to the trench directing they spray against the wall surface.

If there is a concrete or masonry apron around the building, approximately 12 mm (0.5") diameter holes shall be drilled as close as possible to the plinth wall about 300 mm (12") apart, deep enough to reach the soil below and the chemical emulsion pumped into these holes to soak the soil below at the rate of 5 litres per linear metre.

In case of R.C.C. framed structures, the soil (backfill) in contact with the column sides and plinth beams along the external perimeter of the building shall be treated with chemical emulsion at the rate of 15 liters/sq m of the vertical surfaces of the structure. To facilitate this treatment trenches shall be excavated equal to the width of a shovel exposing the sides of the column and plinth beams up to a depth of 500 mm (20") or up to the bottom of the plinth beam if this level is less than 500 mm (20"). The chemical emulsion shall be sprayed on the back-fill earth as it is returned into the trench directing the spray against the concrete surface of the beam or column as the case may be.

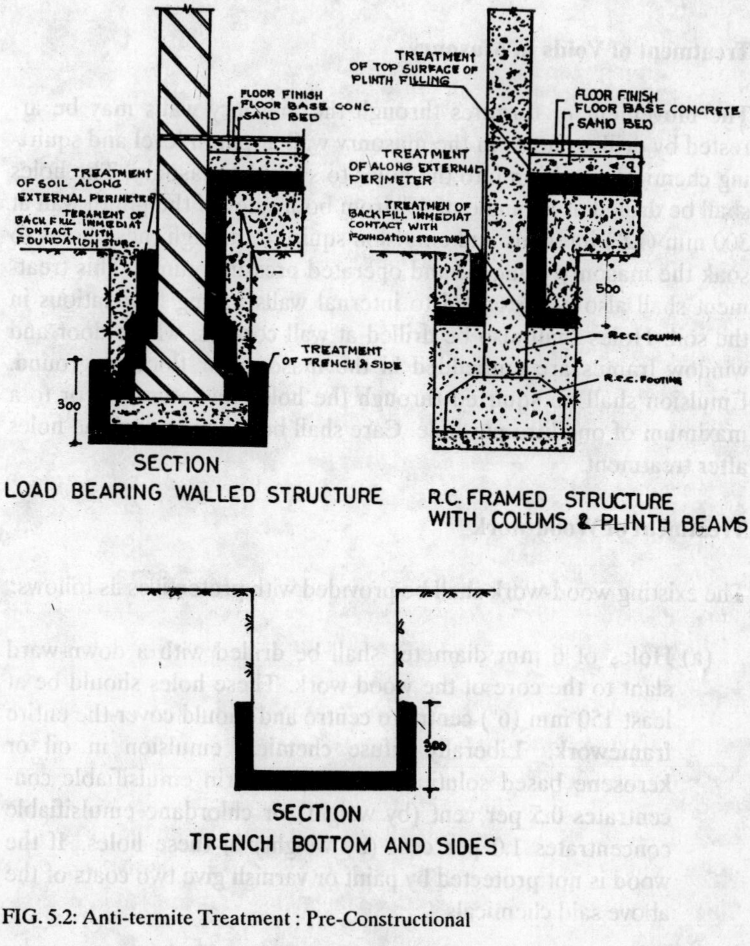

FIG. 5.2: Anti-termite Treatment : Pre-Constructional

Treatment of Soil under Floors

Chemical treatment shall be done by drilling 12 mm (0.5") holes at the junction of floor and walls along the cracks on the floor and along the constructional joints at intervals of 300 mm (12") to reach the soil below. The chemical emulsion squirted into these holes using a hand operated pressure pump to soak the soil below until refusal or up to a maximum of one litre per hole. The holes shall then be sealed properly with cement mortar 1: 2 (1 cement: 2 coarse sand) finished to match the existing floors. The cement mortar applied shall be cured for at least 10 days as per instructions of Engineering-Charge.

Treatment of Voids in Masonry

The movement of termites through the masonry walls may be arrested by drilling holes in the masonry wall at plinth level and squirting chemical emulsion into the holes to soak the masonry. The holes shall be drilled at an angle of 45° from both sides of the plinth wall at 300 mm (12") intervals and emulsion squirted through these holes to soak the masonry using a hand operated pressure pump. This treatment shall also be extended to internal walls having foundations in the soil. Holes shall also be drilled at wall corners, where door and window frames are embedded in the masonry or floor at ground. Emulsion shall be squirted through the holes till saturation or to a maximum of one litre per hole. Care shall be taken to seal the holes after treatment.

Treatment of Wood-work

The existing wood-work shall be provided with protectives as follows:

(a) Holes of 6 mm diameter shall be drilled with a down-ward slant to the core of the wood-work. These holes should be at least 150 mm (6") centre to centre and should cover the entire framework. Liberally infuse chemical emulsion in oil or kerosene based solution of either dieldrin emulsifiable concentrates 0.5 per cent (by weight) or chlordane emulsifiable concentrates 1.0 per cent (by weight) in these holes. If the wood is not protected by paint or varnish give two coats of the above said chemicals.

(b) Spray or infuse all the wood surrounding the masonry with one of the above chemicals.

Optimal and Scientific Use

The old building is most likely not put to on optimal use. The Principal never applies his mind to the question how it can be put to better use. Once he starts thinking on these lines, he may like to take some of the following steps:

(a) *Better Ventilation and Doors*

In most of the old buildings two defects are obvious. First the rooms have poor ventilation so that light and fresh air is scanty. Secondly, doors, specially of class-rooms are of smaller size. Sometimes even in big rooms, there is only one or two doors. This defect must be set right.

(b) *Teacher's Platform*

In most of the class-room, teacher's seat and that of students are at the same level. This is not proper. A small platform should be provided if possible, in the class-rooms so that even if a teacher is teaching while sitting, he can keep an eye on his class.

(c) *Teachers Rota or Desk*

If a teachers wants to teach while standing, he finds that the height of the table is lower and he experiences difficulty in reading his class Attendance register, the text-books, or his notes. So, he should be provided with a Rota or a Desk.

(d) *Black Boards*

The Principal might note that either the size of the Black Boards is not sufficient to meet the requirement of the class held in that room, or it is not properly painted, or its height is not proper. So, he should take remedial measures:

i) The Black-Boards should be got painted every year. There is a special paint for the purpose. The finish should be rough.

ii) New Black Boards with cement can be got prepared.

iii) The classes of Mathematics, Physics, Chemistry, Zoology, Botany, Economics, i.e., needing bigger Boards should be shifted to those class-rooms which have bigger Black-Boards.

iv) The height of the bottom of the Black Board should not be less than 4'3" so that teacher may not have to bend very low. Similarly, the height of the Black Board above 8 feet is a waste. The length may vary between 8′ to 15′.

(e) *Placement of Classes*

Often it is seen that class-rooms are allotted without findings out a co-relation with the strength of the class and size of the class-room. Small classes are put in big rooms and *vice versa*. This is not conducive to discipline and efficient teaching. Rooms should be allotted so that optimal use of the space is done.

It will be advisable that each section of a class is allotted rooms adjacent to each other so that there is minimum of students movements.

(f) *Laboratories*

The laboratories of all subjects, as far as possible, should be so reorganised that they may come at one place. This will be good from safety point of view and also for optimal use of water, electricity, gas, apparatus, etc.

As far as possible in laboratories the ventilation should be maximised. Further, doors must be widened and more doors for entrance and emergency exit be provided.

Gas extinguishers be also provided.

II.
NEW BUILDINGS

The planning of a college campus is a multifarious activity and involves the role of the Management and Principal of the college, educational experts and technical planners. If a new college is to be started or expansion of the existing college is to be made, then the Management of the college, the Principal and educational experts have to take a decision as to what type of courses or facilities the college is going to offer. This decision is to be taken on long-term basis say a period of 10 years and development plan is drawn up stating clearly the growth plan of the college as well as, if possible, the phases of growth. This is a very important decision and has to be taken carefully as it will determine the building requirements.

1. **Manpower**

The college should have a separate set up consisting of technical persons to plan and execute the new buildings. It should resemble the one given earlier for the maintenance of the existing buildings.

2. **Building Requirements**

When the decision about the growth plan of the college has been taken then the building requirements of the college can be worked out. Generally the buildings are required for the following activities:

a) *Administration:* It may include office of the Principal, Management Committee, Admission and Examination cells, Proctors office, etc.
b) *Department of Faculty:* It may include the different teaching departments for the college as well as laboratories.
c) *Lecture Rooms:* It will include all types of lecture rooms.
d) *Library*
e) *Students centre:* It may include girls and boys common rooms, canteen, NCC and Games, stationery and book-shop, post-office, Bank, toilets, etc.
f) *Auditorium*
g) *Health centre*
h) *Cycle and scooter parking*
i) *Play grounds*

The area requirements for the above activities will depend upon the number of students and number of classes in the college. Therefore Master plan for the existing and proposed buildings should be prepared. Again, it should be on long term basis, say a period of 10 years. It is better to include a professional person (Engineer or Architect) at this stage in the planning committee. Many people consider the services of a professional as a financial burden, but in reality it is not so and the remuneration paid to the professional saves many times in the construction costs.

The areas of rooms for activities mentioned from (a) to (i) can be taken from the standards prepared by the various agencies or building by-laws of local authorities. Some recommended norms for a few types of buildings are given in Appendix I.

3. How to locate a New Building?

It has been observed that when a new building — a set of class rooms, a laboratory, a staff room, or any other building is constructed, no serious thought is given to its location. It is necessary that such a mistake should be avoided. Here are some hints for locating a new building:

1. Get a Master plan of the college campus prepared showing all the existing buildings, roads, electric mains, sewage line, etc. This Master Plan should be readily available.
2. The proposed building should form an integral unit with the existing building. Locating it too far from the existing buildings will increase the cost of services like roads and electricity, water and sewage lines.
3. The proposed buildings, as far as possible, should be in continuation with the existing similar building.
4. The site of the building should not be low lying and or water logged.
5. The building should be located well away from main highway and rail track as they will create too much noise and may even create cracks in the building.
6. The site should not be infested with termites. If so, then proper treatment against termite should be given (see Appendix IV).
7. The site should not have any high tension overhead electric line or water or sewage line underneath.
8. The plinth level of the building be such that enough slope is available for the sanitary lines from the building to the discharge point.

4. Economy in Planning of Spaces

The area of different types of spaces can be determined from any of the prescribed norms. However, the economy in spaces can be achieved if spaces for similar types of activities are grouped together in a building so as to reduce the circulation area (Fig. 5.3). For instance there can be one building housing all administrative spaces, one building for departments — this can be split into two buildings, departments requiring laboratories, e.g., Physics, Chemistry, Zoology, Botany, Geology, Geography, Psychology, etc., and the departments which do not require laboratories, e.g., Languages, Social Science, Commerce, Law, etc.

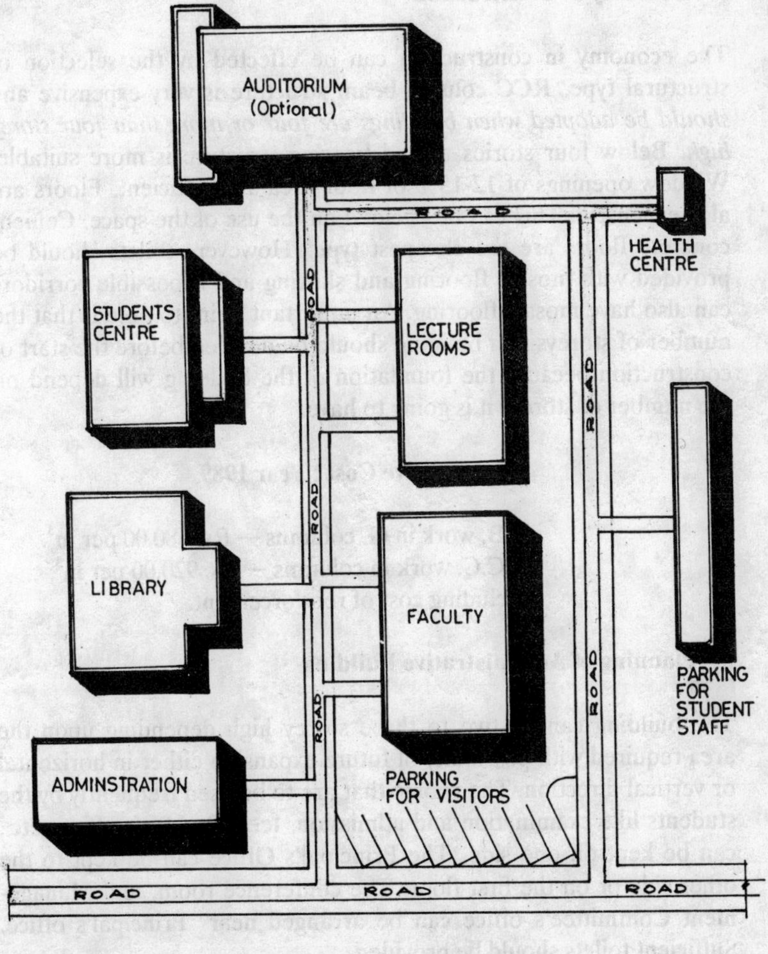

FIG. 5.3: Suggested Lay-out of Different Buildings

The lecture rooms can also be grouped together in a building on the same line as the departments. The students amenities can be grouped in one building while library, auditorium can be separate buildings.

All these buildings together will form the college campus plan and the buildings should be so arranged that the road lengths connecting different buildings are minimum. This will reduce the cost of making roads as well as sewage and water lines.

5. Economy in Construction

The economy in construction can be effected by the selection of structural type. RCC column beam structure is very expensive and *should be adopted when buildings are four or more than four storey high.* Below four stories a load bearing structure is more suitable. Window openings of 12-15% of floor area are sufficient. Floors are also expensive. This can be decided on the use of the space. Cement concrete floors are the cheapest type. However, toilets should be provided with mosaic flooring and skirting and if possible corridors can also have mosaic flooring. An important point to note is that the number of storeys in a building should be decided before the start of construction because the foundation of the building will depend on the number of storeys it is going to have.

Comparative Cost : Year 1989

R.B. work in G. columns — Rs. 680.00 per m^3.
R.C.C. work in columns — Rs. 920.00 per m^3.
excluding cost of reinforcement.

6. Planning of Administrative Building

The building can be two to three storey high depending upon the area required with possibility of future expansion either in horizontal or vertical direction. The rooms that are to be used frequently by the students like examination and admission, fees, Proctor's office, etc., can be kept on one side. The Principal's Office can be kept to the other side or on the first floor. The conference room, and Management Committee's office can be arranged near Principal's office. Sufficient toilets should be provided.

7. Building for Departments

These can be grouped into departments with laboratories and without laboratories. The space requirement for department would be an office for the Head of the Department, space for office assistant, store, laboratory space and rooms for staff members. Since the National Policy on Education, 1986, emphasises on programmes of teacher orientation and continuing education, effort should be made to provide a room for every two or three staff members. An ideal case would be one room for one teacher. A tea room can be provided which can also be used for departmental meetings. To economise on space one tea room can be provided for three or four departments together. Sufficient toilets as required should also be provided.

8. Lecture Rooms

The space area for lecture rooms can be decided upon the number of students it is going to accommodate. This is a matter to be decided by educational planners. A width of 6-7 metres for lecture rooms will be more suitable. The ratio of length and width should normally be 2:3. Lighting should be sufficient. Light over Black Boards is very useful. A raised platform near the Black Board for the teacher is an added advantage. It increases the visibility of Black Board to students. There is no need to provide toilets in lecture room blocks as these will be provided in the students' centre.

9. Library

There should be an independent library for the whole college. The areas of spaces for different activities can be calculated on the basis of prescribed norms. The planning of library is a highly professional work. The important points to observe are that stack rooms should have proper ventilation and air circulation so that books are not spoiled. Reading rooms can be separated for undergraduate, postgraduate and staff members. Sufficient toilets for both boys and girls should also be provided (see Chapter on Library).

10. Students' Centre

In vacant periods, the students will be spending their time here. Therefore it should have common rooms separately for boys and girls with toilet facilities. It would also have a canteen. Other student related activities like NCC, games, post-office, Bank, stationery and book shop can also be located in this building. If a separate health centre is not provided, then a dispensary can also be provided in this building. The building should be one or two storey high with possibility of future expansion.

11. Auditorium

The building for auditorium should be very carefully decided by the Principal and Management of the college. It is the most expensive structure and very sparingly used and requires large sum of money in furnishing and recurring maintenance. Most of the colleges cannot afford it. However, its need is felt when there are functions like cultural programmes, convocation, public lectures, etc. Small colleges can go in for semi-permanent structure (skeleton frame is errected permanently which is covered whenever required).

Hindu College, Delhi (old building at Kashmiri Gate) had invented a working auditorium for lectures and debates. It was a well type structure with steps. On each step, students seats were provided. The area was covered with a tin shed which rested on pillars. The stage was on the first step, which was higher than the ground floor. It could accommodate about 500 students. A rough sketch is provided in Fig. 5.4.

Large colleges can build a multi-purpose hall which can be used for cultural activities, sports, examinations and admissions. A large part of the hall should be left without fixed seatings which can be used for other activities. If the auditorium is in use for the whole year then it should be built otherwise there is not point in spending scarce resources.

12. Health Clinic

For colleges having residential facilities for students and teachers a separate unit with 2 or 3 beds should be provided. For colleges without residential facilities a dispensary would be sufficient.

13. Parking for Cars, Scooters and Cycles

Sufficient parking space should be provided for cycles, scooters and cars. It should be at one place and near the entrance.

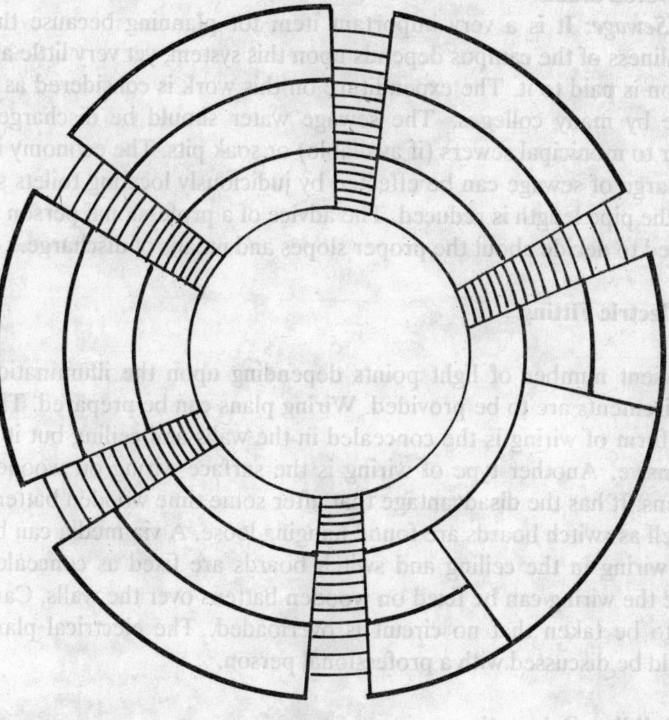

FIG. 5.4: Rough Sketch of an Auditorium

14. Water Supply

To have good water pressure an overhead tank of required capacity either on independent staging or at the highest level in a building is suitable. The tank can be filled either through an independent tube-well or municipal water collected in an underground tank. The capacity of the tank and its staging height can be determined on the basis of the number of users and laboratories and water consumption standards (Appendix II).

15. Rainwater and Sewage Drainage System

(a) *Rain Water:* Adequate care should be taken to drain off the rain water from buildings and its surroundings. Adequate number of rain water pipes should be provided in the building to drain the roof water. It can then be carried to municipal drain either through open or covered drains.

(b) *Sewage:* It is a very important item for planning because the cleanliness of the campus depends upon this system, yet very little attention is paid to it. The expenditure on this work is considered as a waste by many colleges. The sewage water should be discharged either to municipal sewers (if available) or soak pits. The economy in discharge of sewage can be effected by judiciously locating toilets so that the pipe length is reduced. The advice of a professional person is needed to decide about the proper slopes and means of discharge.

16. Electric Fitting

Sufficient number of light points depending upon the illumination requirements are to be provided. Wiring plans can be prepared. The best form of wiring is the concealed in the walls and ceiling but it is expensive. Another type of wiring is the surface wiring on wooden battens. It has the disadvantage that after some time wooden battens as well as switch boards are found hanging loose. A via media can be that wiring in the ceiling and switch boards are fixed as concealed while the wiring can be fixed on wooden battens over the walls. Care has to be taken that no circuit is overloaded. The electrical plans should be discussed with a professional person.

17. Building Orientation

South east or east light should be secured for as many rooms as possible. South light is satisfactory if east or south east light cannot be obtained.

Buildings should be set away from street approximately 20 to 30 metres. Open areas will be required around the buildings.

18. Appraisal of Plans prepared by Architects/Engineer

The appraisal of plans prepared by architects or engineers is the essence of planning. The appraisal team should include the actual users of the building. The appraisal team should scrutinise the plans and see if the building would serve their long-term needs. If changes are required at this stage then they should be done.

19. Anti-Termite Treatment

(See Appendix IV)

APPENDIX I

(A)

Norms and Standards for the College Building in Delhi

The panel on University Building examining the norms and standards for college buildings recommends that the accommodation that may be provided for various purposes in the College buildings to be constructed in Delhi be as follows:

I. *Lecture Rooms*

(a) To seat 100 students —	2 @ 10 sft. (0.93 sqm) (per student)	2,000 sft. (186 sqm)
(b) To seat 75 students —	6 @ 10 sft. (per student)	4,500 sft. (418 sqm)
(c) To seat 40 students —	6 @ 12 sft. (1.15 sqm) per student	2,880 sft.
(d) To seat 15 students —	10 @ 15 sft. (1.40 sqm) per student	2,250 sft. (210 sqm)

In the case of colleges having B.Sc. classes also, the number of Lecture rooms of 75 students may be reduced from 6 to 4 as a similar number (two) is provided for with the Science Laboratories.

II. *Teachers' Rooms Blocks*

50 rooms with an area up to 100 sft. (9.3 sqm) each to be built in stages. Twenty rooms at the first stage and the remaining to be provided as the staff increases the rooms to be used as sitting-cum-small tutorial rooms. 2,000 sft. (186 sqm)

III. *Administration*

(i) Principal's room attached with a bath room, PA's room and a retiring room	600 sft. (55.75 sqm)
(ii) Bursar's room	150 sft. (14 sqm)
(iii) Office	600 sft. (55.75 sqm)
(iv) Office records & stationery	500 sft. (46.45 sqm)
(v) Stores (General)	800 sft. (74 sqm)
(vi) Staff Common room for teachers	600 sft. (55.75 sqm)
(vii) Common room for Boys	500 sft. (46.45 sqm)

(viii) Common room for girls	250 sft. (23.22 sqm)
(ix) In case where only one common room is to be provided for Boys or Girls	600 sft. (55.75 sqm
(x) Canteen including N.R.S. Centre	1,600 sft. (148 sqm)
(xi) Sports Store	500 sft. (46.45 sqm)

IV. Auditorium for 600 students @ 7 sft. (0.655 sqm) per students with a proper projection room and stage which should be designed for amateur college plays but total floor area including stage lobbies etc., may be between 5,500 sq. ft. (511 sqm) and built up area may not exceed 7,500 sft. (696.75 sqm).

V. *B.Sc. Laboratories for Physics/Chemistry*

Physics — 40 students

(1) Main Laboratory	1,200 sft. (111.50 sqm)
(2) Electricity-cum-Dark Room	600 sft. (55.75 sqm)
(3) Store Room	400 sft. (37.15 sqm)
(4) Preparation Room	300 sft. (27.85 sqm)

Chemistry — 40 Students

(1) Main Laboratory	1,600 sft. (148 sqm)
(2) Balance Room	300 sft. (27.87 sqm)
(3) Store Room .	400 sft. (37.15 sqm)
(4) Preparation Room	300 sft. (27.85 sqm)

VI. *Common Facilities*

(1) Gas House	500 sft. (46.45 sqm)
(2) Workshop	600 sft. (55.75 sqm)
(3) Lecture theaters (to seat 75 students each @ 12 sft. per student)	1,800 sft. (167.20 sqm)

VII. *Health Centre* (for check-up purposes only)

VIII. *Small Gymnasium*

IX. Accommodation for N.C.C.

Accommodation to be provided for the last three (VII, VIII, and IX) will be determined in consultation with appropriate authorities.

The accommodation recommended above is for a total strength of 1,000 students and if in a particular case a college decides to reduce the maximum number of students that may be enrolled, suitable prorata modifications may have to be made.

The accommodation except that of the auditorium is indicated in terms of carpet area and can be converted into built up area under the usual formula, i.e. by additing 50% of the corresponding carpet area.

(B)
Standards for Library Buildings and Design

Based on IS 1553-1976 — Indian Standard recommendation relating to Primary elements in the Design of Library Buildings. (First revision)

1. *Location* — The library should be centrally located with reference to buildings of faculties and departments, laboratories and hostels.
2. Rooms to be provided are as follows:

Sl. No.	Rooms normally separate	Academic library	
		UCL*	UDL**
a)	Stack room	R	—
b)	Catalogue room	R	—
c)	General reading room	R	R
d)	Periodical reading room	R	—
e)	Special reading room	R	—
f)	Research cubicles	R	—
g)	Group study room	R	—
h)	Seminar room	R	—
i)	Conference room	R	—
k)	Librarian's room	R	—
l)	Dy. Librarian's room	R	—
m)	Technical staff room	R	—
n)	Administrative staff room	R	—
o)	Committee room	R	—
p)	Display room	R	—
q)	Night watchman's room	R	—
r)	Microfilm reading room	R	—
s)	Document reproduction room	R	—
t)	Audio visual room	R	—
u)	Store room	R	R

* University Central Library
** University/College Department Library

Each unit rack 2 m long may be assumed to house 700 volumes and 1 m^2 of stock room area may be assumed to house 150 volumes.

Note: 1. The centre to centre distance between consecutive racks is 1.80 m (on the basis of 0.45 m) of rack depth plus 1.35m of cross gangway width).

2. The distance from an end wall of the stack room to the centre of the nearest row of rack is 1.55 m (on the basis of 1.325 m of the end cross gangway plus 0.225 m of half rack depth).

3. **Stack Room**

3.1 Dimensions of stack room should be as follows:

a) Clear length in metres — 1.80n+3.10 where *n* is the number rows of book racks.

b) Clear width — (1) 3m (on the basis of one rack 2 m long plus on longitudinal gangway of 1 m) close to a longitudinal wall.

2. (2) 5 m (on the basis of 2 rack each 2 m long plus longitudinal gangway of 1 m) close to a longitudinal wall.

(3) 8 m (on the basis of 3 racks each 2 m long plus two longitudinal gangways of 1 m each) close to each of the longitudinal walls and;

(4) 10 m (on the basis of 4 racks each 2 m long plus two longitudinal gangways of 1 m each) close to each of the longitudinal walls.

Notes: Three metres and five metres widths are generally provided in case of stack spaces, as the stack room and the reading room may be combined into a single room in such cases.

(c) *Clear Height* — Floors to ceiling 2.40 m.

Note 1. The height of the rack is 2.20 m and allowance for day guides is 0.20 m.

2. The stack room should be combined with necessary devices for effective ventilation.

3.2 Stack room should be so oriented as to avoid direct sun.

4. **Windows**

4.1 Stack room window in the side walls of the stack room should be opposite each cross gangway.

4.2 Each window should be provided with glass shutters and

protected with wire fabric having its aperture sufficiently small to prevent squirrels, bats, etc., from getting in. In its fully open position the glass shutter should not project into the gangway.

4.3 *Other rooms* — All window and ventilators in the rooms accessible from outside should be provided with wire fabric to prevent books pamphlets, etc., being taken out through them.

5. Sizes of Rooms

5.1 *Reading room* — The average area per reader in the reading room should be 2.33 m^2 minimum. An illustrative layout of the reading room is shown in Fig. 5.5.

Note: The size of the reading table is 2X4X0.6 m the centre to centre distance between two consecutive rows of reading room tables is 1.8 m with seating arrangement on one side of the table only.

5.2 *Sizes of other room* shall normally be as follows:

For use of	Area m^2
a) Librarian and Dy. Librarlan	30
b) Classifier, cataloguer, acession librarian and maintenance librarian	9 per person
c) Secretary to the librarian	9
d) Visitor's room	15
e) Administrative and professional staff not at service points and other than those mentioned in (b)	5 per person
f) Groups discussion room	15 per person
g) Conference room	40 per person
h) Seminar room	20 per person
i) Committee room	20 per person
j) Cubicles	7 per person

6. *Libraries* of all types are expanding at an enormous rate. Increase in demand for documents, official policy and increase in literacy make this process inevitable. Since the development of new libraries take several years the stock to be accommodate on the opening day, therefore, will be large than was estimated when planning started. Therefore, it is absolutely essential to estimate the areas of the library at a given future date and relate the requirement to that date.

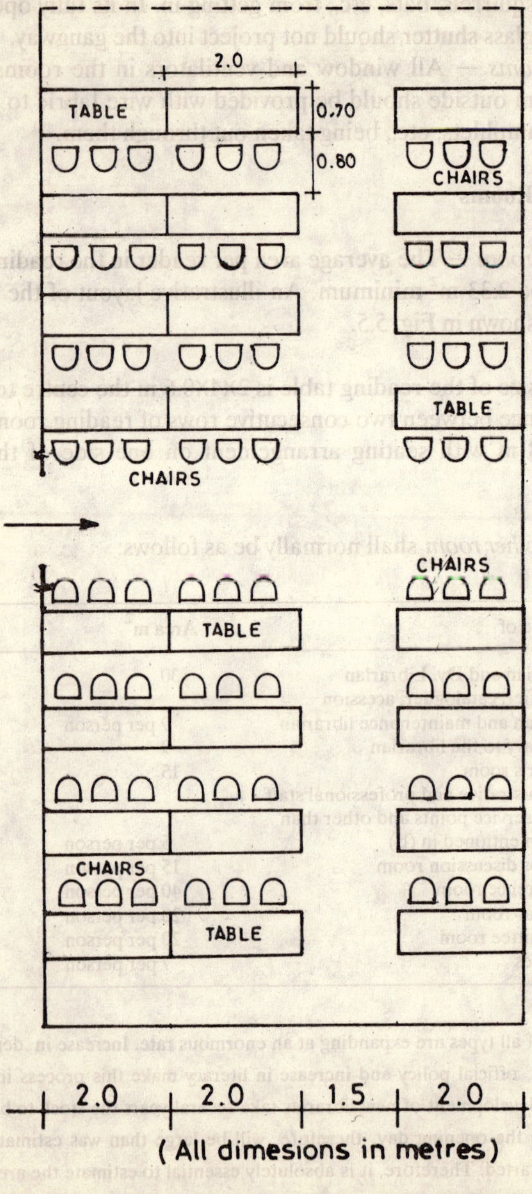

FIG. 5.5: Layout of Reading Room

7. **Circulation**

7.1 Each floor of the library building shall be at one single level to facilitate the movement of book trolley from one part to another. Thresholds shall not be provided any where in the building.

7.1.1 The movement of the book trolley from one tier to another where there are three or more tiers in the stack room should be through electric lifts provided within the stackroom with landing at every tier of the stackroom and at other connected adjacent rooms. In large libraries where quick mechanical carriage of books and related materials are required, special arrangement, such as pnequmatic tubes and belt conveyors may become necessary. This needs be considered at the initial stages of design of the library and its building.

7.1.2 The rooms shall be arranged in such a way that the staff other than those servicing the reading room shall not have to pass through the reading room disturbing the readers.

8. **Relative Positions of Rooms**

8.1 The stack room should be so placed that it is easily accessible from and proximate to every part of the library.

8.2 The catalogue room should be like an ante-room on the way from the general reading room to the stack room.

8.3 The general reading room should be close too the entrance.

8.4 Periodicals' rooms may be further removed from the general reading room. But independent access to it shall be possible when the other rooms in the library are closed.

8.5 Special reading rooms may be still further removed from the general reading room.

8.6 The librarian or deputy librarian should have his room in close proximity to the general reading room.

8.7 The rooms of the technical and administrative staff should be placed in close proximity to the rooms of the librarian and the Dy. Librarian.

8.8 The technical staff shall have independent access to the stack and catalogue areas.

8.9 The cubicles, the rooms for group study, the committee room, may be a in a separate wing or a separate floor.

8.10 The exhibition room may be combined with the entrance lobby or placed as close to it as possible.

9. The furniture and fittings for library shall be as per IS: 1829 (Part I and II) and IS Library furniture and fittings Part I timber (First revision) and Part II steel and IS: 3663-1981 dimensions for rigid couplings, tables and chairs for general office purpose.
10. Requirement for fitment for drainage and sanitation for library building shall be as per the Appendix III.

(C)
Hostels (Up to four storeys)

1. *Orientation* — The blocks should be so oriented that the living rooms get sufficient day light, natural ventilation and better comfort conditions. In this reference be made to IS 76626 (Part I) — 1974, IS 2440–75 and IS-3362–77.* The following climatological factors may also be taken into account for better orientation and internal environment:

   Solar radiation and temperature
   Rainfall
   Wind direction
   Humanity

2. *Living Room* — The optimum space requirements for a living room in a hostel for graduate level will have the following parameters:
   Single seated accommodation 8-9 sq.m per student
   Double seated accommodation 7.5 to 8 sq.m per student
   Triple seated accommodation 7-7.5 sq.m per student
   The areas of room for post graduate level will not exceed 10 sq.m
3. *Kitchen and Dining* — The dining area shall be determined at the rate of 1 sq. ft per diner. The space shall be provided for 50 per cent of the strength of the Hostel subject to a minimum of 40 sq.m. The kitchen area shall be provided at the rate of 5.5 sq. ft. (0.5 m^2) per diner subject to a minimum of 60 sq.m. The kitchen area shall be provided with the facilities of water tapes and locker. Cooking arrangements can also be provided within the norms at the choice of the University/College. Fuel yard shall be provided

---

* Bureau of Indian Standards, Manak Bhawan, 9 Bahadur Shah Zaffar Marg, New Delhi-110002.

near the kitchen.

The Dining and Kitchen space shall be provided with the following :

Toilet facilities for diners:

Less than 100 diners

Urinals	3
Wash basin	5
W.C.	1

More than 100 diners

Urinals	6
Wash Basin	8
W.C.	1

The floors of the dining and kitchen space shall be finished with terrazzo and dedo up to sill level. All doors and windows will be provided with fly-mesh shutters.

4. *Common Room:* The common room space shall be provided for 25 per cent of hotel strength at the rate of 2 sq. mt. per user up to a minimum of 60 m^2. The common room accommodation shall be provided preferably on the ground floor and as far as possible near the dinning space so that these facilities could be combined when required. There is no need of providing a separate laboratory in case the common room is near the dining space.
5. *Toilet Facilities* The toilet unit will have the following facilities :

W.C.	1 for every 10 students 1 for every 8 women/girl student
Urinal	1 for 20-25 students
Wash basin	1 for 8-10 students
Shower	1 for 8-10 students.

Based on above norm provisions, an areas of 0.7 m^2 per student is adequate for toilet. W.C. should normally be of Indian type but one toilet of European type may be provided in special circumstances. A small storage space for brooms, floor brushes, etc., shall be provided within the toilet block. The location of the block shall be so marked that the bad smell is not carried to living accommodation through the prevailing breeze. Provision of exhaust fan may also be made in each toilet block. Provision may be made for hot water supply in regions where necessary.

6. *Area of Openings* — The area of openings excluding doors and ventilators shall lie between 12 to 15 per cent of the floor area.
7. *Total floor Area:* An overall area of 17 m^2 per hostler including circulation will be adequate. This includes living rooms circulation space, wall area, service area and common room but it does not include Dining and Kitchen areas.
8. *Provision of Services* — The following provision shall be made for water supply, sanitation and electrification while determining the cost of the hostel.

Internal water supply and sanitation	7-1/2 of total cost of civil works
Internal electrification	10% of total cost of civil works without fans
	12-1/2% of total cost of civil works with fans.

9. *Furniture* - - The following furniture shall be provided in each room of the hostel per student:
   Cot/Reading table/chair/tea table—one each.
10. *Warden's Office* — 80 to 90 ft (7.5 to 8.4 m^2) of office accommodation shall be provided for the office of the Warden.
11. *Furniture Store* — Furniture store of 160 to 180 sq.ft. (15 to 17m^2) shall be provided for extra/repairable furnitures.
12. *Parking Space* — A separate covered space at a convenient location shall be provided for cycle and scooter parking at the rate of 1.8 m^2 per cycle/scooter for 35 per cent of the strength of the hostlers.
13. *Drinking Water* — Adequate space for water coolers at convenient locations shall be planned for installation of water coolers in future when funds are available.
14. *Circulation Space* — Attempts should be made to keep the circulation area to the minimum. It should be around 25 per cent of the total plinth area excluding the area for stair case. Hostels are planned either with central corridor or passage on one side. Though the Central corridor system is economical but it is often not feasible because of inadequate natural lighting, cross ventilation and noise level. The width of Central corridor should not be less than 5′-0" (1.5 m). However, for singly loaded corridor it could be 4′-2" (1.2m) only. The location of stair cases and toilet

blocks shall be such that the walking distance from the farthest room is within 100 ft (30 m) the width of the stair case flight should be 4′ (120 cm) clear.

Note: 1. The planning efficiency shall be achieved to the maximum by functionally grouping together various activity spaces. Preferably the total built up areas should be 2.3 to 2.5 times the total living unit area.

2. A room with an area of 22.5 m^2 may be provided for the guest and relatives of the students coming from out stations, the space shall be provided to accommodate at least three guests at a time.

(D)
Teachers Hostels (Up to 4 storey)

(1) *Space requirements*

a) For single occupancy 40 m^2

b) For married couples 60 m^2

In addition circulation and common facilities may be provided @ 20 m^2 per unit.

General — Requirements for fitments for drainage and sanitation may be added (see NBC 1983 Part IX Sec.) or IS 1172-1983 Code of Basic Requirements for Water Supply Drainage & Sanitation (Third Revision).

(E)
Accommodation for Staff Quarters

Accommodation	*Plinth area*
(a) Type-I : Professor/Readers House/flats	Basic structure 150 m^2

Note: : Houses/flats may be built with servants quarters and garage.

(b) Type-II : Lecturer's quarters 100 m^2

Note: House/flats may be built with 4 m^2 scooter shed.

Note. Where only one watercloset is provided the bath and watercloset shall be separately accommodated. Water closet unless indicated otherwise shall be of Indian Standard (Squating type).

(F)
Norms and Standards for Construction of Guest House

Guest House

i)	Single rooms (with attached bathroom)	8
ii)	Double rooms	4
iii)	VIP suit	1
iv)	Lounge (with attached toilet)	1
v)	Dining room, kitchen, pantry, etc.	1 each
vi)	Small office cum reception	1

The areas for the above purpose may be as follows:

	Living area plus accommodation for Bath room, W.C., Entrance, Lobby, Dressing	Total
i)	Single room 12 m^2 + 8 m^2	200 sq.ft.
ii)	Double room 20 m^2 + 10 m^2	300 sq.ft.
iii)	VIP Suit 88 m^2 + 12 m^2 (This will consist of one bed room plus one sitting room)	400 sq.ft.
iv)	Lounge with attached toilet 800 sq.ft. (600 + 200 sq.ft)	
v)	Indoor games and Reading room	600 sq.ft.
vi)	Dining room (with facilities for 25 persons dining at a time)	300 sq.ft.
vii)	Kitchen, pantry, etc.	250 sq.ft.
viii)	Small office-cum-reception	150 sq.ft.
ix)	Store and Linen room	150 sq.ft.

(G)
Space Norms for Health Centre

Sl.No.	Name of facility	No. of rooms	Size	Area in sq.m.
Out Patients				
a)	Consultation & Examination	2	4X3.5m	14 sq.m
b)	Dispensary	1	3.5X2.5m	8.75 sq.m
c)	Dressing	1	4X3.5m	14 sq.m
In Patient				
a)	Ward area/2 bed ward	—	3.5X3.5m	12.25 sq.m
b)	Ward area/4 bed ward	—	6.0X3.5m	21.00 sq.m
c)	Attendants room	3	3X2.5mX7.5sq.m	18.75 sq.m each
Common and Ancilliary				
a)	Laboratory	1	2.5X3.5m	
b)	X-ray with dark room and store	1	7.0X3.5m	24.5 sq.m
c)	Operation room with sterilization and scrubup	1	5.0X3.5m	17.5 sq.m
d)	Preparation room	1	3X3.5m	10.5 sq.m
e)	Labour room/delivery	1	4X3.5m	14.00 sq.m
f)	Office room with storage	1	4X3.5m	14.00 sq.m
g)	Store			
	i) Medicine	1	4X3.5m	14 sq.m
	ii) Linen & Equipment	1	4X3.5m	14 sq.m
	iii) General	1	3X2.5m	7.5 sq.m
h)	Garrage for Ambulance	1	5.5X3.5m	19.25 sq.m
i)	MCH & FP	1	5.5X3.5m	19.25 sq.m
j)	MCH room with exam.	1	5.5X3.0m	16.5 sq.m
k)	Toilet and urine testing shelf purpose cum F.P.		3.5X7.5m	26.25 sq.m
Waiting				
a)	Consultation & Examination		10 persons	
b)	Dispensary & Dressing	1	10 persons	50 sq.m
c)	Operation & Labour		4 persons	
d)	MCH		5 persons	

Toilets	W.C.	Urinal	Wash basin
Public			
Male	1	2	1
Female	1	1	1
Wards			
Male	1	1	1
Female	1	–	1
Staff			
Male	1	1	1
Female	1	–	1

The size shall be in accordance with the norm recommended by National Building Code.

Note: 1. To start with provision of only 6 beds may be made. The facility for provision of more beds will depend upon the size of the University and other local needs.

2. The overall plinth area of the Health Centre including of the area for circulation, services and wall are a may not exceed 600 sq.m.

APPENDIX II

Water Requirements for Buildings

Sl. No.	Type of Building	Consumption of per head per day (Litres)
1.	Hostel	135
2.	Offices	45
3.	Restaurants (per seat)	70
4.	Auditoriums	15
5.	Day college	45
6.	Boarding College	135

APPENDIX III

Water Supply, Drainage and Sanitation

Based on IS 1972-1983 Indian Standard Code of Basic Retirements for Water Supply, Drainage and Sanitation (Third Revision).

ART GALLARIES, LIBRARIES & MUSEUMS

Sl. No.	Item	For Male public	For Female public	For Male Staff	For Female Staff
1.	2	3	4	5	6
1.	Water closets	1 per 200 persons up to 400 persons; and for over 400 persons, add at the rate of 1 per 250 persons or part there of	1 per 100 persons up to 200 persons; and for over 200 persons add at the rate of 1 per 150 persons or part there of	1 for 1 to 15 persons 2 for 16 to 35 persons	1 for 1 to 12 persons 2 for 13 to 25 persons
2.	Addition taps	1 in each water closet	1 in each water closet	1 in each water closet	1 in each water closet
	Note: 1 water tap with draining arrangements shall be provided for every 50 persons or part thereof in the vicinity or water closet and urinals.				
3.	Urinals	1 per 50 persons	1 per 50	Nil up to 6 persons 1 for 7 to 20 persons, 2 to 2 to 45 persons	
4.	Wash Basins	1 for every 200 persons or part there-of and for over 400 per-sons add at the rate of 1 per 250 persons or part thereof	1 for every 200 persons or part there of and for over 200 per-sons add at the rate of 1 per 150 persons or part thereof	1 for 1 to 15 persons 2 for 15 to 35 persons	1 for 1 to 12 persons 2 for 12 to 25 persons
5.	Cleaner's sinks	———	1 per floor	Min———	———
6.	Drinking water foundation	———	1 per 100 persons or part part thereof	———	———

APPENDIX IV

Anti-Termite Treatment : New Building

3. *Pre-construction Chemical Treatment* — This is a process in which chemical treatment is applied to a building in the early stages of its construction.
   Hand operated pressure pumps shall be used for uniform spraying of the chemical. To have proper check for uniform spraying of chemical, graduated containers shall be used. Proper check should be kept that the specified quantity of chemical is used for the required area during the operation.
4. *Time of application* — Soil treatment should start when foundation trenches and pits are ready to take mass concrete in foundations. Laying of mass concrete should start when the chemical emulsion has been absorbed by the soil and the surface is quite dry. Treatment should not be carried out when it is raining or soil is wet with rain or sub-soil water. The foregoing applies also in the case of treatment to the filled earth surface within the plinth before laying the sub-grade for the floor.
5. *Disturbance* — The treated soil barriers shall not be disturbed after they are formed. If by chance, treated soil barriers are disturbed, immediate steps shall be taken to restore the continuity and completeness of the barriers system.
6. *Treatment for Column-pits, Wall-trenches and Basement Excavations:*

   (a) The bottom surface and the sides (up to a height of about 300 mm) of the excavations made for column pits, wall trenches and basements shall be treated with the chemical at the rate of 5 litres per sq.m of the surface area (see fig.5.2).

   (b) After the column foundations and the retaining wall of the basement come up the backfil in immediate contact with the foundation structure shall be treated at the rate of 15 litre per sq.m of the vertical surface of the sub-structure for each side. If water is used for ramming the earth fill, the chemical treatment shall be carried out after the ramming operation is done by rodding the earth at 150 mm centres close to the wall surface and spraying the chemical with the above dose. The earth is usually returned in layers and the treatment shall be carried out in similar stages. The chemical emulsion shall be directed towards the concrete or masonry surfaces of the columns and wall so that the earth in contact with these surfaces is well treated with the chemical.

(c) In the case of R.C.C. framed structures with column and plinth beams and R.C.C. basements the concrete mix is rich and dense (being 1 : 2 : 4 or richer), it is unnecessary to start the treatment from the bottom of excavations for column and plinth beams. The treatment shall start at the depth of 500 mm below ground level. From this depth the back-fill around the columns, beams and R.C.C. basement walls shall be treated at the rate of 15 litres/sqm. of the vertical surface. The other details of treatment shall be as laid down in clause (b) above.

7. *Treatment of Top Surface of Plinth Filling*: The top surface of the filled earth within plinth walls shall be treated with chemical emulsion at the rate of 5 litres per sqm. of the surface before the sand/sub-grade is laid. Holes up to 50 to 75 mm deep at 150 mm centres both ways shall be made with crow bars on the surface to facilitate saturation of the soil with chemical emulsion.
8. *Treatment of Junction of Wall and Floor*: To achieve continuity of the vertical chemical barrier on inner wall surfaces from the ground level, small channel 30X30mm shall be made at all the junctions of wall and columns with the floor (before laying the sub-grade) and rod holes made in the channel up to ground level 150 mm apart and the chemical emulsion poured along the channel @ 15 litre per sq.m of the vertical wall or column surface so as to soak the soil right to bottom. The soil shall be tamped back into place after this operation.
9. *Treatment of Soil along External Perimeter of Building*: After the building is complete, provide holes in the soil with iron rods along the external perimeter of the building at intervals of about 150 mm and depth 300 mm and filling these holes with chemical emulsion at the rate of 5 litres per meter of perimeter of the external wall.
10. *Treatment for Expansion Joints*: Anti-termite treatment shall be supplemented by treating through the expansion joint after the sub-grade has been laid @ 2 litre per linear metre of expansion joint.
11. *Treatment of Soil Surrounding Pipes and Conduits*: When pipes

and conduits enter the soil inside the area of the foundations, the soil surrounding the points of entry shall be loosened around each such pipe or conduit for a distance of 150 mm and to a depth of 75 mm before treatment is commenced. When they enter the soil external to the foundations, they shall be similarly treated unless they stand clear of the walls of the building by about 75 mm for distance of over 300 mm ground level.

12. *Safety Precautions*: All chemicals used for anti-termite treatment are poisonous and hazardous to health. These chemicals can have an adverse effect upon health when absorbed through the skin, inhaled as vapours or spray mists or swallowed. Person using or handling these chemicals should be warned of these dangers and advised that absorption through the skin is the most likely source of accident poisoning. They should be cautioned to observe carefully the safety precautions give below:

These chemicals are usually brought to site in the form of emulsifiable concentrates. The containers should be clearly labelled and should be stored carefully so that children and pet cannot get at them. They should be kept securely closed.

Particular care should be taken to prevent skin contact with concentrates. Prolonged exposure to dilute emulsions should also be avoided. Workers should wear clean clothing and should wash thoroughly with soap and water, especially before eating and smoking. In the event of severe contamination, clothing should be removed at once and the skin washed with soap and water. If chemicals splash into the eyes they shall be flushed with plenty of soap and water and immediate medical attention should be sought.

The concentrates are oil solutions and present a fire hazard owing to the use of petroleum solvents. Flames should not be allowed during mixing.

Care should be take in the application of chemicals to see that they are not allowed to contaminate wells or springs which serve as sources of drinking water.

6

ADMISSION POLICY

Admissions are the first step of the ladder leading to taking the college to the stage of being called an elite college. So, a Principal should pay maximum attention to the framing of Admission Policy. Here are certain points which he should deliberate upon before finalising his policy.

1. **Quantity** vs. **Quality**

Various Education Commissions have recommended that a college should not have more than 1000 students or so on its rolls. The U.G.C. funding policy of college shows that bulk of the colleges have a strength of less than 500 students and a very few have a strength of more than 3000 students.

A Principal should fix up the number of admissions in each class on the basis of number of subject teachers, i.e., the number of maximum subject periods they can taken, number of class rooms, furniture in the class rooms, etc. Normally, he should insist that a section will not have more than 60 students because thereafter it becomes a crowd and ceases to be a class. As far ass possible, he should resist the temptation of running the college in shifts.

The Government, for the Past forty years, has been insisting on mass education at the cost of quality of education. So, the Principal will have to decide how much he will be able to resist the demand of increasing the enrolment of the college and fix it as per his infrastructure.

In some States such as U.P., the Government pays the salaries of the approved staff and leaves only 20 per cent to 25 per cent of the fees to the colleges to meet all other expenses such as maintenance and white-washing of buildings, furniture, electricity, stationery, chalk, duster and Attendance Registers, etc. If the admissions are reduced then the 20 or 25 per cent money left to meet all these expenses, which are daily increasing due to cost excalation, will be miserably insufficient. So, a balance is to be struck. How much admissions should be reduced or increased will depend upon this financial constraint.

2. Educational Background

It is a well-established fact that there is a marked difference in intelligence quotient, way of thinking and behaviour, among students coming from educated parents and uneducated parents, from cities and villages, from business class families or service class families. So, the Principal should decide his admission policy with a view to which section of the society he primarily proposes to cater. His admission policy should reflect it.

Under the prevalent conditions, a Principal has not much scope to select students from a particular group of families. So, he should try to club students of different backgrounds in different sections so that he can organise teaching of different sections differently.

3. Scheduled Castes and Scheduled Tribes

As per Government rules, a Principal has to admit a certain percentage of S.C. and S.T. students, if they are available and they fulfil the minimum eligibility conditions. So, there is not much choice here.

It is now being increasingly felt that the academic performance of S.C. and S.T. candidates is generally not up to the mark. A survey conducted by the author revealed that most of the S.C. and S.T. candidates came from half a dozen scheduled castes out of 67 castes in U.P. They have psychological complexes. They are not regular nor serious about studies. They are quick at picking up quarrels on trifling pretexts.

When a Principal admits such students up to one-fifth of the college strength, naturally he should frame his admission policy in such a way that he can pick up the best out of them. Further, as a follow up action, the Principal should take some concrete steps to remove their complexes and make them more study-oriented.

4. Mixed Institution

If the college is not only a girls' college or only a boys' college but is a mixed institution, then the question to be debated upon is the ratio of male and female students to be admitted. There is no such restrictions imposed by the Government or the University. So it can be only an internal decision of the college.

Past experience shows that the girl students are better at studies, they are not a discipline problem by themselves, due to cultural traditions these girl students live in small groups and feel suffocated, there are sex scandals and they become an extra problem when any law and order problem suddenly crops up. The Principal should take all these and many other factors into consideration before fixing the ratio of girl and boy students. Probably, it will be better if ratio is low at undergraduate level and high at post graduate level.

The author of these lines, after assuming the charge of Principalship, formulated an admission policy for his college. Every factor was quantified so that the total marks of student applicant can be calculated. On the basis of these total marks, the merit lists and waiting lists were prepared and admissions were given exclusively on merit.

To make the scheme successful, admission committees, Faculty wise, were formed. They were given detailed instructions, full freedom and supporting staff. The last date for applying was fixed. Thereafter, students on the basis of merit were called for personal interview. About 50 student per day were called for one class. Information was sent by post.

A discipline committee of teachers was formed to guide and help new students who had come to take admission.

This procedure was time consuming but it gave excellent results. Indirectly, it raised the creditability of the college in the eyes of citizens. Further, as the years rolled on the rules were edited in the light of experience.

After a few years, the author was made the chairman of the Admission Committee of the University. These admission rules framed by the college were passed on to the university Admission Committee for consideration. The University, thereafter, made detailed admission rules for all colleges and enforced them. However, the University failed to exercise a control to ensure strict adherence to the rules.

The Norms of Admission

It is a matter of common experience that usually in most of the institutions admission are not made on merit. Therefore, norms, which may be almost the same for all classes should be ventured.

These norms should be divided into two parts;

1. General
2. Particular — Faculty-wise and class-wise.

Here, the norms for university classes will be discussed which, with slight modifications, can be applied to other stages of education also.

1. *General Norms*

i) Every institution should publish a prospectus the price of which should be the same for all similar institutions and should be fixed by the university concerned. This prospectus should give, besides other things, the admission norms and procedures, the details of fees, other important rules and formalities such as the last date for applying, etc. The prospectus should have an application form and other forms such as Library membership form, Proctor's office record form, N.C.C. form, fee concession forms, etc.

ii) The admission to be made to the various classes and also in various subjects of each class should be fixed on the basis of the availability of teachers, optimum strength of each section of a class, size of class rooms, class furniture, size and equipment of laboratories, library facilities, etc. This class-wise and subject-wise strength should be approved, on the basis of the relevant data, by the affiliating university.

iii) The admissions should be purely on the basis of merit which should be determined by the particular norms prescribed Faculty-wise. However, admission should be refused to the following categories of applicants even if they are eligible for admissions otherwise:

(a) If the gap between the last examination passed and the class to which admission is sought is more than 5 years. However, a relaxation can be made at the discretion of the Head of the institution who will reduce it to writing, giving the justification. It will be better if marks are deducted at the rate of 2 marks per year's gap.

(b) If a student has failed in the class to which he is seeking admission in more than two attempts.
(c) If he has been punished by a criminal court for some crime (excluding minor crimes such as rash driving).
(d) If an F.I.R. has been filed which implicates him for heinous crimes.
(e) If he has been guilty of indiscipline in any institution earlier.
(f) If the head of the institution has other reasons to refuse him admission. Thcy must be reduced to writing.

(iv) Weightage in admissions shall be given to players, office bearers of the Students' Unions, N.C.C. 'C' certificate holders, N.S.S. camp certificate holders, wards of soldiers and freedom fighters, wards of teaching and non-teaching staff of the institution.
(v) A merit list together with a waiting list should be prepared for each class. The applicants should be informed through the prospectus itself, to see the Notice Board on the fixed dates (one date for merit list and the next date for waiting list) and complete the formalities of admissions within the next seven days. The seats left vacant from merit list should be filled in from the waiting list in order of merit.
(vi) Usually no change in subjects should be allowed.

Particular Norms — Faculty-wise

The relative merit of applicants to a particular class, can be mathematically worked out. This calculation procedure shall vary from class to class and Faculty to Faculty. With a view to demonstrate the feasibility of making such calculations, a few illustrations can be ventured:

A. **For Faculty of Arts and Commerce**

(a) *Under-graduate class*

i) Percentage of marks secured in High School or equivalent examination.
ii) Percentage of marks secured in Intermediate or equivalent examination.

(b) *Post-graduate class*

i) One-fourth of the percentage of marks secured in High School or equivalent examination.
ii) One-fourth of the percentage of marks secured in Intermediate or equivalent examination.
iii) Half of the percentage of marks secured in first degree examination.
iv) Ten per cent of the marks secured in B.A./B.Com in the subject in which admission is being sought in M.A./M.Com.
v) Three marks for being student of the college at first degree level or two marks for being the student of the same university.

(B) **For Faculty of Science**

(a) *Under-Graduate-Class*

i) Percentage of marks secured in High School or equivalent examination.
ii) Percentage of marks secured in Intermediate or equivalent examination.

(b) *Post-graduate class*

i) One-fourth of the percentage of marks secured in High school or equivalent examination.
ii) One-fourth of the percentage of marks secured in Intermediate or equivalent examination.
iii) Half of the percentage of marks secured in B.Sc.
iv) Three marks for being student of the college at first degree level or two marks for being a student of the same university.

Note: No application will be deemed eligible for admission in a subject at M.Sc. level if he has not secured atleast 50 per cent marks in that subject at B.Sc. level.

One cannot dispute that such mathematicalisation of admission norms will leave no scope for elasticity and sometimes there might be casualties of hard case. One way to meet this criticism is to authorise the Head of the institution to grant admission to the maximum of 10 cases in a year with a provision that he will have to reduce to writing the justification for granting the admission out of merit. These exceptions will be subjected to scrutiny by a Board to be nominated by the concerned university.

It is not claimed that these norms of admissions are perfect in themselves. They can be taken only as a starting point and should be perfected on the basis of experience and demands of the time. However, intentions should be good and noble.

(C) Faculty of Education

Some universities are holding entrance examination for B.Ed. courses. So, there is hardly any need to formulate admission rules for the colleges affiliated to such universities. But for other colleges, norms can be something like below:

1. *Merit Count should be:*

High School	15% of percentage of marks secured
Intermediate	25% of percentage of marks secured
B.A./B.Sc.	40% of percentage of marks secured
M.A./M.Sc.	20% of percentage of marks secured

2. *Additional Counts*

University product	10 points
N.C.C. 'C' or 'G' certificate	6 points
N.S.S. camp @ 2 per camp	6 points Max.
Scout masters Training course	6 points
Sons and daughters of Army Personnel	5 points
Games University or zone level player	6 points

3. *Teaching Experience*

For every year 2 marks	6 points

Faculty of Law

Competitive entrance examinations are being held. Hence, no need to formulate norms.

7

SOME THOUGHTS ON LABORATORIES AND PRACTICAL WORK *

"Good teachers are the first requirement, the *sine qua non.* But we must certainly put the necessary equipment as the second requirement."

— *H.F. Boulind*

Science courses are different from the other courses for the fact that here the theories are accompanied or followed by practical work with apparatus, equipments and materials. A considerable part of the time spent in learning science has to be used for experimental work. Hence, there is a need for well equipped laboratory. the word 'laboratory' generally means a room or building providing opportunity for (especially scientific) research, experimentation, observation, or practice in a field of study. Laboratory is supposed to be the life and blood of a particular course. It should provide an environment congenial to learning science. Here, the students should receive not only the knowledge of science and its application; but also acquire better understanding of science and its application. Laboratories should provide all sorts of educative experiences relating to science. If these are not located at a proper place, equipped adequately and manned by competent staff, the very purpose of the laboratories will be lost.

Present Day Position

1. As a result of population explosion in our country and greater public awakening towards education, the number of can-

---

* This chapter is based mainly on the observations of college laboratories of U.P. The conditions in rest of India are almost the same. The difference is in degrees alone.

didates seeking admission to higher classes is increasing every year. The colleges are helpless and unable to provide admission to all in under-graduate and post-graduate courses. Normally, out of the total students who apply for admission to science classes only one-third are successful.

2. The criterion of the admission is, or should be the merit counts, calculated on the basis of the percentage of marks obtained by the candidate in 10 and +2 or intermediate examinations. (Irrespective of whether the percentage is genuine, or obtained as a result of mass copying).
3. It is a common practice in the colleges to admit more students than the seats fixed by the Govt/Universities. The Principals do not stick to the admission rules. They are under the pressure of Members of the Managing Committee of the college, local political leaders and student leaders. These admission are done violating the admission rules framed by the universities. Thus, sub-standard students get admission.
4. The direct effect of this admission is that the laboratories become overcrowded. Normally, 60-70 students are kept in a group for practicals when the laboratories can hardly accommodate 50 students.
5. The result of this overcrowding is that in the laboratories, the students are doing their practical work not individually but in small groups. One student is doing the work and the remaining 4 or 5 students are satisfied by watching it.
6. The same sight is seen in the balance room of the chemical laboratory.
7. It will not be an exaggeration in saying that majority of the students, coming from Intermediate colleges, have poor equipment. Most of them have never handled even the balance. It is more true for the boys coming from rural areas.
8. It is quite impossible for the teachers present in the laboratory, because of the strength of 60-70 students, even to correct the students' record-books, not to say of going from seat to seat and removing the students difficulties. This will naturally reflect on the academic standards.
9. In the chemical laboratories the reagent bottles are not in sufficient number and are normally kept far away from the working place. The result is that the students roam about in the laboratory in search of desired reagent bottles. Valuable time is unnecessarily lost in this *"searching bottle"* exercise.

10. Faced with these limitations the teachers lose interest and prefer to remain sitting and gossiping. It is a common sight in most of the college laboratories.
11. Equipment, apparatus, chemicals and other material always remain in short supply, and the supplied one is of very sub-standard quality. Measuring flasks, pipettes, burettes and other glass apparatus are not precisely calibrated. The weights in the weight boxes do not give the correct weight of the substance, being weighed.
12. Knowing fully well the standard of the material being supplied to the students for their practical work, teachers don't pay any attention towards the results obtained by the students on the assigned task. While correcting the record book teachers only write 'high' or 'low' about the correctness of the result.
13. Due to paucity of chemicals, very diluted solutions of the reagents are prepared which do not give the desired results. Even for the practical examinations, the reagents of optimum, concentrations are not prepared. Teachers faced with this reality pay hardly any attention when the reagents are being prepared by the concerned laboratory assistant.
14. The material to the laboratories is not supplied regularly. No provision is made for repairing of the apparatus and instruments. There is no recurring grant in the departments for maintenance with the result that the life of the apparatus and material is shortened. After sometime, such apparatus is dumped in the stores and concerned practical exercise is deleted from the list. Whenever new grant in the name of the department of under-graduate or post-graduate classes is received from U.G.C., the new apparatus is again purchased. After the use of this new apparatus for a few years this also meets the same fate and the cycle is repeated again. A lot of such dumped apparatus can be seen in the stores of different deptts. of the colleges.
15. The teachers are not happy with this state of affair prevailing in the science laboratories of our degree colleges. From time to time they even try to draw the attention of college Principal and Secretary, Managing Committee towards the rapidly deteriorating working conditions. At the state level and UGC level also, Teachers Associations have raised these issues. It is unfortunate that except assurances, nothing happens.
16. The result is that the teachers have now compromised with the

prevailing situation. They have become indifferent. They are just passing the time outside as well as inside the laboratories and the academic standards are falling.

17. There is not much to do for the teachers in the laboratories. So they have directed their time and energy in different productive means such as business, coaching, private tuitions and minting money.
18. In colleges the conditions have come to a stage where more than one fourth of the students are taking private tuitions paying Rs. 300-400 per subject per month. The parents and students have lost their faith in the college education.
19. It seems that our Government has taken a policy decision to produce as many science graduates as possible without taking care about the quality of education and standard of science graduates. There is no cell, panel or committee to monitor the working conditions of the laboratories of the degree colleges. It is thought that till the work is going on peacefully it is allright. When there is some agitation, the Government loses no time in appointing a committee or commission. The appointment of a committee or commission, it is increasingly realised, is a technique to pass time and pacify agitators.
20. Acquiring of scientific knowledge and scientific outlook are the two main objectives of science teaching. These can be achieved only through regular practical work in the laboratory. A student inside the laboratory should not be a passive observer but an active worker, an enthusiastic experimenter and a discoverer in the making. This is possible only when adequate equipment, apparatus and other material of right quality are made available.
21. One of the most important and time consuming aspect of science teaching is the selection, procurement and care for apparatus and equipment. Selection of the material may be made by a panel of teachers in each department. As there is no dearth of good, committed and dedicated teachers, such teachers may be appointed as members of the panel. After selecting right type of material as per need, this panel should frame proposals for the new academic year at least six months before the start of the next academic session furnishing full details. The Heads of the department along with Principal and one or two senior members should scrutinise the proposals within a maximum period of two months. The sanctioning

authority must accord the sanction immediately, so that the departments after completing the formalities may place the orders for the material and procure them in time before the new session starts.

22. In actual practice, the sanctioning authorities accord the sanction for the purchase of material when the examinations are near at hand. This takes place in the month of February and March when all purchases are to be finished by the end of March. It causes and unusual demand for science material. The result is that the materials required are not available. As a result of this, the colleges go in for poor quality of material at higher cost. A number of malpractices also spring up such as adjustment of predated bills without receipt of materials.
23. At present teachers of the departments have no say for planning and selecting the materials.

Finances

1. Most of the colleges do not have enough resources at their disposal to meet the normal expenditure of the department. It is quite impossible to run the college laboratories in a meaningful manner on the monthly fees of the students and on the insufficient grant or aid given by the Govt./U.G.C.
2. The grant received from the Govt./U.G.C. is not in proportion to the number of students admitted in different classes by the college.
3. Escalation of prices of materials due to inflation has made it all the more difficult for the college Managing committee and Principal to run the laboratories properly.

   There seems to be an immediate need to raise the monthly fees charged from the students to an optimum level so that the colleges may become self reliant.

Remedies

1. The enrolment to B.Sc. and M.Sc. classes should be curbed. Only 'really' interested and well deserving students be given admission as per resources of the department.
2. Hackneyed and stereotype exercises in practicals may be deleted from the syllabus. In this rapidly changing world of science, attention should be given to instrumentation

wherever required. New exercises of more importance and utility should find place in the syllabus. In the beginning more funds will be needed, but in the long run these exercises will prove more economical.

3. In view of making higher education self sufficient the science fees may be raised substantially. Once the fees is raised,the colleges will not only become self reliant, the crowd of non-deserving, undesirable and less interested students will be checked. However, to help meritorious poor students, fee concessions may be given by the Govt. instead of subsidising the college fees, the better way is to grant full freeships to poor meritorious students.
4. Enhanced fees will also check the menace of private tuitions taken by the students.
5. Due to enhanced fees the parents will become serious and will take interest in the regular studies of their wards. There will be awakening in the students towards their studies. Then, it will also be possible to fix the responsibility on the teachers.
6. In the field of higher education there should not be any religion or caste based reservation of any kind. The first and foremost priority for the admission should be the student's own merit.

Some More Suggestions

Keeping into consideration the importance of laboratories, the following suggestions can also be ventured:

1. It will be profitable, if all the college laboratories, particularly the laboratories of the science subjects, are brought in one building or in a continuous block. It will, besides economy, ensure better water and electric supply and more safety. It will save time of students and teachers also in moving from one laboratory to another. It will also facilitate pooling of technical staff in times of emergency or better coordination for full utilisation of limited staff. It may facilitate in installation of a generator in these times of electricity shortages and failures.
2. In one block-building, the under-graduate labs may be clubbed, subject-wise, at one place and similarly the post-graduate labs and Research labs at another place.
3. At Post-graduate and Research level there are several com-

mon apparatus/equipment which are required in different subjects. These include electrical balances, thermostat, oven, spectrometer, refrigerator, barometer, cameras and costly microscopes, *etc.* For such equipment a separate room be provided adjacent to the Post-graduate and Research labs. This room be called *'Basic Instruments Lab'*. It should be manned by one Lab. Asstt., one Lab boy and one electrician-cum-technician. This arrangement will not only economise in the purchase of instruments/equipments but will also ensure their proper maintenance and maximum use.

4. With the *'Basic Instrument Lab'* a cubical should be attached which may be used for repairing the apparatus/equipment. The provision of such a workshop exists for the Post-graduate Deptt. of Physics. This repairing workshop should be manned by a qualified and competent person and the basic machines like drill, lathe, etc., should be provided. Voltameter, ammeter, batteries, balances, chokes, etc., can be repaired and maintained in this workshop. It will prove both economical and efficient.
5. Every university prescribes the number of students of a batch. The size of the laboratories should be such that it may accommodated at least two batches at a time. It will still be better if one laboratory can accommodate all the students of one section, where number should be the multiple of the strength of a batch.

   In this lab, separate cubicles be provided for teaching and non-teaching staff.

   The face of the laboratories should be towards east so that even when electricity fails, the students, may get sufficient light and air.

   Each laboratory, specially the chemistry one, should have exhaust fans.
6. The design of furniture and electric fittings should be as per need of the subject laboratory. It is essential to associate faculty members of the subject while planning the building, equipping it, designing the electric fittings and furniture, *etc.*
7. Most of the college Labs. work with coal gas or oil gas. These days commercial Gas cylinders are available with Indian Oil Co. They work out to be cheaper and safer.
8. A Central Purchase committee consisting of two senior teachers from each department under the Chairmanship of

the Principal of the college should be constituted. The guiding principles of the purchases be formulated and strictly adhered to. One such principle should be that only the best quality equipment and apparatus be purchased from standard suppliers, preferably from manufactures.

9. It will be a sound policy to get the following things completed during summer vacations:

   a) Stock taking and weeding out irreparable things.
   b) Repairing of equipment, apparatus, furniture, etc.
   c) Plan purchases for the next session and place orders.
   d) Do all those things which are for the good of laboratory.

10. Efforts be made to eliminate wasteful expenditure and innovate new methods of teaching.
11. The State Government and Director of Higher Education should be approached:

    a) To revise the norms for sanctioning non-teaching posts. For example, a post of clerk-cum-store keeper is essential for each science subject. Again a post of a curator and a helper for each of the museums of the Deptts. of Zoology, Botany and Geology is a must. Similarly, a post of a Seminar librarian in each post-graduate science subject is a necessity.
    b) To revise the minimum qualifications, requirements, etc., of non-teaching staff associated with science labs.
    c) To revise the science lab. fees. The present fees is insufficient. It should be appreciably raised.

12. The U.G.C., C.S.I.R., D.S.T., etc., should be approached to make it obligatory that retired Professors, who are granted Research Projects will have to associate themselves with a college (not with a university) so that the college subject labs may become enriched and the experience of these senior teachers be utilised by the colleges in improving their teaching and research.

8

COLLEGE LIBRARIES : A Few Guidelines

A college library is a place where books, journals, magazines, newspapers and other materials are collected, housed and provided to the readers as per their needs. Here the reading material is scientifically arranged and displayed so that it may be easily available to the readers. It is a nerve centre which supplements the class room teaching and is an aid to the readers to help themselves in developing their mind and get better informed and equipped.

Some experts opine that a college library is like a beacon light from which academic light emanates. If it functions well, it can be presumed that the college is functioning well. And when colleges are functioning well, the future of the country is bright because, after all the alumni of the colleges are the future guardians of the country.

The college library purchases books, magazines, journals and periodicals, displays and issues them to the readers. They may be classified as below:

1. *Reference Books* – Rare books and journals on different subjects, Dictionaries and Encyclopaedias, Biographies including Autobiographies, Ph.D. Theses and M.A. dissertations, Parliament and State legislatures Reports, General knowledge books, costly maps (Geography, History, other sciences, etc.).

2. *Books* – Subject books prescribed in various courses, standard books of these subjects, important general books for recreational reading, *etc.*

3. *Periodicals, Newspapers, Magazines, etc.*

4. *Pamphlets, Booklets, Monograms, etc.*

5. *Government Publications*.

6. *Audio-visual materials*.

In ancient India *Gurukulas* had excellent libraries. For example, Nalanda and Takshila were famous for their rich libraries. It is unfortunate that foreign invaders destroyed these priceless collections. Thereafter, in Mughal period, *Madarsas* and *Pathshalas* never tried to build libraries. This indifference to libraries continued even in the British days as they were not interested in really educating slave Indians. They wanted them to become, at best, clerks. The Calcutta Education Commission (Sadler Commission), established in 1917, has this to say:

> "Few colleges have good libraries. Even the best as that of the Presidency College, is very defective at many points."

The Radhakrishnan Commission on Higher Education paints the following picture of college and university libraries:

> "While at a few universities the libraries are fairly well stocked, grants for their upkeep are more or less reasonable, arrangements for lending books to teachers and students are efficient and the reading space is reasonably adequate. *It was distressing to find that in most colleges and universities the library facilities are very poor indeed.*"

It can be said, without the fear of contradiction, that the condition of the college libraries was poor in pre-independence days and it is not very different even today in spite of all tall claims. For example, S.R. Ranganathan, a great librarian, described the position of college libraries over a half century ago in the following words:

> "College library consisted of closed cupboards. Most of them were concentrated in one or two rooms called general library. Hardly any student cared to go to the general library. A student could at best reach up to the barrier, select all by himself a title from a tattered volume of printed catalogue and drop an application form for it into a tray, one morning each week. By the evening, the available books would all stand piled up in the pile, but he would often feel disappointed by the book not suiting his standard or by being something different from what he thought it to be."

Even today the conditions have not much improved due to the several reason enumerated below:

(a) There is an explosion of literature, information and knowledge. The doubling rate in science subjects was 30 to 40 years but the rate at present is about 5 to 8 years. In certain subjects like chemistry and space science, the growth rate is even faster. The college libraries are not able to grow with the same speed for want of resources and various other reasons.

(b) Because of the policy of the government and also the natural desire of people, the demand for higher education is increasing. Libraries are not able to keep pace with this growing enrolment and the consequent pressure of demands for library facilities.

(c) Prices are rising quite fast but the cost of publications is rising faster. So, with limited funds, libraries are not able to acquire even the essential books and periodicals and thus acquire lesser number of books and other reading material.

(d) The trained and untrained staff required to run a college library is not available.

(e) The building, furniture, modern technical gadgets, *etc*., required to run a college library are not available.

(f) Method of teaching and evaluation in colleges is so defective that there is no incentive or competitive spirit aroused among students to go to library and try to equip themselves better.

(g) No guidance is provided to college students on how to make use of college library.

** ** **

The vital role college libraries should play in higher education has been well recognised by our educationists, librarians, education commissions and committees, planners, and by all other concerned with the growth and development of higher education in the country, particularly during the post independence era. Radhakrishnan in 'University Education Report (1950)' said:

> "The library is the heart of all the university's work directly as regards its research work, and indirectly as regards its educational work which derives its life from research work. Scientific research needs a library as well as its laboratories, while for humanistic research the library is both library and laboratory in one. Training

in higher branches of learning and research is mainly a question of learning how to use the tools, and if the library tools are nor there, how can the students learn to use them."

The Government of India established the University Grants Commission (UGC) in the year 1953. However, the Parliament passed an act to that effect in the year 1956. The Commission during the Chairmanship of Dr. C.D. Deshmukh took keen interest in the development of university and college libraries. A committee under the Chairmanship of Dr. S.R. Ranganathan was appointed to advise the UGC about the development of libraries. Some of the recommendations of the committees were:

i) The entire library finance of a University or a college library should be provided by the Commission and the State Government;
ii) For the time being, the Commission's share may be four-fifths of the total requirement and the share of the State Government may be the remaining one-fifth;
iii) The Commission should not ordinarily withdraw or lower its grant to a University or a college library because the State Government fails to provide the corresponding matching share;
iv) Subject to local variation, the capacity of the university to spend and the amount at the disposal of the commission for grant for reading and kindred materials, Rs. 15 per capita on the basis of students registered in the university and Rs. 200 per teacher may be given as grant to a university library for the time being. These figures should be revised periodically in the light of the changes in the cost of books and periodicals;
v) The library grant in any year should be based on the statistics data of the preceding year;
vi) The status and the salary scales of the library staff should be the same as those of the teaching and research staff. In other words, the college library should be considered as an academic unit and not as an administrative or ministerial unit.
vii) In a small college with an annual book fund of less than Rs. 20,000 the librarian should be in grade 3, i.e., University

lecturer with the qualifications appropriate to it;

viii) In a large college with annual book fund of not less than Rs. 20,000 the librarian should be in grade 2, i.e, University Reader with qualifications appropriate to it;

ix) The standards for the library building, fittings and furniture, established by Indian Standards Institute should be followed; and

x) Any proposal, for new library buildings, fittings and furniture, or for the adaptation of any existing building, or for its extension for library purposes, should be examined and approved by a library expert appointed by UGC.

The Kothari Commission on Education in its report presented in 1966 endorsed the same emphasis on the importance of libraries:

> "No university, college or department should be set up without taking into account its library needs in terms of staff, books, journals, space, etc. Nothing could be more damaging to a growing department than to neglect its library or to give it a low priority."

With this importance of college library, it become essential for a Principal to know several things which are necessary for the development of the library. Here are a few of them.

I. BUILDING

The requirements of a library building are different from those of other buildings of the college, some of the important things are:

a) The library building should be located at a place which is away from the hustle and bustle of college activity. At the sametime it should not be that far away as students and teachers may feel inconvenience in going there.

b) The college library is a growing institution. So, the building should be so planned that it can be expanded both horizontally and vertically. It should have strong foundations so as to bear load of a multi-storied building.

c) No room or Hall of the college library should have direct sun rays as they are injurious to paper of books, journals, etc.

d) There must be lot of circulation of fresh air.

e) The application of anti-termite be made (see chapter on building)

f) The walls should be free from dampness. Fool proof arrangements should be made against water leakage. It will be advisable to mix damp proof chemicals in the mortar meant for plasters. Other treatments should also be done. It is desirable that humidity should not be more than 45°.

g) Safeguards against rats, squirrels, etc., be taken. As far as possible the water outlets must be covered with nets.

h) It is desirable that the room temperature should not be more than 25°C, Air coolers should not be fixed because they increase humidity. It is difficult to instal Air conditioners. So, lot of greenery be provided all around the library. It will give it a glamour also.

i) As far as possible concealed wiring of very superior quality be used to avoid short circuiting and fire.

j) The space, in a college library, for different uses should depend upon a number of factors, *viz.*, number of students, number of volumes, facilities offered to reading public, *etc.* Some standard specifications are :

i) Reading Room	2.33 m^2 per reader — it is advisable to provide space for 25% students on rolls and 50% of teachers.
ii) Study Space	2.75 m^2 per student.
iii) Research and teachers	3.3 m^2 per scholar.

In 1986, the U.G.C. released the latest document titled 'Recommendations made by the University Grants Commission for different types of buildings'. It will be profitable to consult it.

Indian Standards Institute, New Delhi has prescribed library Standards, some of which are :

1. Design of Library Building — IS 153-1960

It will be a good idea to entrust the work of library building to a team of qualified architects, structural engineers and college librarian.

II.
FURNITURE

The U.G.C. has laid down some norms of furniture. For example, a library should have the following number of seats:

a) Under-graduate level — 10 to 25% of Enrolment
b) Post-graduate level — 25% of enrolment
c) Ph.D. level — 10% of the strength of research scholars enrolled.

The tables, chairs, news-paper stands, racks, etc., of library are of types different from the common furniture. So, their design, etc., should be taken from standard suppliers.

Indian Standards Institute has prescribed standard specifications in IS 1829, Part I, 1978 and IS 1827 (Part II), 1977.

III.
STAFF

Today college libraries are growing in size and complexity. Books collection in the libraries has multiplied manifolds. The growth in number of students, the introduction of new courses, the constant increases in annual budgets and the frequent special grants from U.G.C. have placed additional and often new demands on college libraries. Together with it, the expectations of the users are rising. They are demanding reference, documentation, bibliographical and reprographic services. To meet all this demand and render efficient services, sufficient staff, both trained and untrained is required.

Our college library staff is inadequate from the point of view of quality and quantity. The academic qualifications possessed by many librarians are not adequate to perform the specialised professional responsibilities. Over and above, they are under-staffed.

1. The U.G.C. has formulated norms for colleges in Delhi. They can be a guide and a starting point. They are :

   a) If a college has 1100 students, the library functions for 7 hours a day and number of books are between 15,000 to 30,000, then the minimum staff requirements are :

i)	Librarian	—	1
ii)	Asst. Librarian	—	1
iii)	Semi Professional Asstt.	—	1
iv)	Jr. clerk	—	2
v)	Attendants	—	2

b) If a library works for 12 hours a day, then 2 more attendants be given.

c) If Post-Graduate classes and Research facility are added, then the minimum staff should be —

i)	Librarian	1
ii)	Asstt. Librarians	2
iii)	S.P.A.	2
iv)	Clerks	2
v)	Attendants	4

2. Some senior librarians feels that the minimum library staff for a college should be

i)	Librarian	1
ii)	Dy. Librarian	1
iii)	Asstt. Librarian	1
iv)	Library Accountant	1
v)	Steno-typist	1
vi)	Correspondence clerk	1
vii)	Attendants	4

3. The ratio between qualified workers and non-qualified ones should be 1 : 3. This includes class IV employees also.
4. As per U.G.C. recommendations, additional staff is required as below:

   a) One person for every 6000 volumes added in a year.
   b) One person for every 500 current periodicals is needed to attend to acquisition work.

5. Work studies show:

   i) one person can do accession of 75 books per day

ii) one person can catalogue 25 books per day
iii) one person can shelve 180 books per day
iv) one person is needed for issuing the books, if the library opens for 15.00 hours per day. However, this norm does not appear to be just because work load of the person will depend upon how many readers get the books issued or returned per day and what other duties are assigned to him.

The strength of staff should depend upon the work load in different sections.

6. Selection, placement sand training play an important role. So honest efforts be made to select the best persons available. It will be desirable to associate librarians of good libraries as experts. The statutory provision of U.P. to associate District Inspectors of Schools, Employment officer or a representative of the Director of Education office is ridiculous.
   Placement should be as per individual specialisation and aptitude.

It is essential that the technical staff is regularly given exposure so that they may know the latest techniques, schemes, ideas, etc. With this added knowledge, they may like to adopt it with necessary modifications in their college library. So, as a habit they may be regularly sent to attend workshops, symposia, conferences and visit good libraries.

The non-technical staff should be encouraged to improve their qualifications. Study leave with the maximum permissible leaves with pay should be granted. The only condition should be that they will come and serve the college for atleast three years.

7. It is always beneficial to try to make the library staff contented and happy. The Principal should

   a) Try to know each and every worker by name and face,
   b) Try to know their personal problems and help in solving them,
   c) Reward the workers for work on holidays, or work for longer hours in a day or for better efficiency,
   d) Punish them only when it has simply become unavoidable,
   e) Implement service conditions liberally.

IV.
FUNDS

No good library can be developed and maintained without adequate funds. An idea of the minimum funds required can be had from the U.G.C. funding of Delhi colleges which are constituent colleges.

1. a) Library fees charged from the students are

   i) Under-graduate — — Rs. 144.00 per annum
   ii) Post-graduate — — Rs. 180.00 per annum

   b) U.G.C. gives a recurring grant between Rs. 15,000.00 and Rs. 20,000.00 p.a. to a college which has an enrolment of approximately 1100 students.

   Thus, a college gets about Rs. 1.70 lakhs p.a. i.e., Rs. 150 per student per year.

2. U.G.C. is giving Book grant to the colleges at the following ratio:

   a) **Under-graduate education**

   i) Small colleges below 500 students — Rs. 1000 per student out of which 20 per cent is for books and journals, i.e, Rs. 200 per student.
   ii) Medium colleges with 1000-2000 students — Rs. 400.00 per student out of which 20 per cent is for books and journals, i.e., Rs. 80 per student.
   iii) Big colleges with 3000 and above student Rs. 100 per student out of which 20 per cent is for books and journals, i.e., Rs. 20 per student.

   b) **Post-graduate Deptt.**: All departments are not eligible, but those that are lucky to have a sanction of Rs. 2 lakhs to Rs. 3 lakhs can spend about Rs. 40,000 on Books and journals. Obviously, these sanctions of the U.G.C. for books and journals are neither sufficient nor rational.

V.
ALLOCATION OF FUNDS

Allocation of limited funds to various subjects and other purposes (Reading Room Papers and Magazines, Reference Section, Reprography section, etc.) is the most difficult task. To avoid pulls and pushes, a scientific formula should be adopted.

Shri R.S. Saxena, the dynamic librarian of the Roorkee University evolved a formula based on the number of students — undergraduate and research, number of teachers and number of subjects. The author of these lines adopted it in his college with certain modifications. It gave optimal results. The formula, besides considering the number of students and teachers, also took note of the prices of books of the various subjects. Normally, the books of Hindi, for example, are cheaper than those of economics or psychology. And the books of subjects in Arts Faculty are cheaper than books of Science subjects. The formula was as under:

Under-Graduate Deptts.

1. Faculty of Arts	Books of Re. 1.00X per student
2. Faculty of Commerce	Books of Re. 1.25X per student
3. Faculty of Science	Books of Rs. 1.50X per student

Post-graduate Deptt.

1. Faculty of Arts	Books of Rs. 1.50X per student
2. Faculty of Commerce	Books of Rs. 1.75X per student
3. Faculty of Law	Books of Rs. 1.75X per student
4. Faculty of Education (B.Ed., M.Ed.)	Books of Rs. 1.75X per student
5. Faculty of Science	Books of Rs. 2.00X per student

Research Students and Teachers

1. Faculty of Arts	Books of Rs. 2X per person
2. Faculty of Commerce	Books of Rs. 2X per person
3. Faculty of Law	Books of Rs. 2X per person
4. Faculty of Education	Books of Rs. 2X per person
5. Faculty of Science	Books of Rs. 2.5X per person

It is easy to calculate the value of X and thereby allot funds to different departments of the college.

This formula gives higher share to Post-graduate Department and also includes Research Students and Teachers. Hence, the funds allotted to a Post-Graduate department and Research students include allocation for Research Journals also.

While calculating the value of X some money should be kept aside for allocating extra grant to newly established departments, Reading Room (purchase of News Papers and Magazines) if no separate fees is charged for R.R., Reference Section (Biographies, Autobiographies, Dictionaries, Encyclopaedias, Govt. Reports, etc.), Reprography Section (Electrostat, Audio-Visual aids, computer, etc.), Health Section (care and Preservation of Books) and emergency expenses.

Since the prices of books and periodicals are continuously rising, yearly allocation of funds for library must also increase proportionately.

VI.
ACQUISITION SECTION

In the modern world there is explosion of knowledge. It is estimated that each year 10 lakh books are added, 80 to 90 thousand periodicals are released, 20 lakh research reports are issued and nearly 30 lakh articles appear in various journals and magazines. How to select the best and the most useful material with the limited resources is a difficult question.

What to purchase and from where to purchase is the task of the Acquisition Section of the library. Obviously, those days are gone when the college librarian alone could do it. Now a team work is needed. More so, because there are pulls and pushes in divergent directions. The various sections of readers — undergraduate students, Post-graduate students, Research students, Teachers, Non-Teachers, members of the Management and sometime people connected with the district administration — all want a priority to be given to them in the matter of feeding their requirements. So, the best course will be to form a small committee with the librarian as ex-officio Secretary. One teacher from each faculty, one seniormost research student, one student from each faculty, (the one who has secured the highest marks) be nominated by the Principal.

Prof. Ranganathan gave two dicta: Every reader his or her books', and, 'Every book must find its readers'. This means that the need of maximum number of readers be met and no useless books should be purchased.

The guideline to purchase various categories of literature can be:

1. Text books — 40% of total allocation
   Normally one text book should be provided for five students. This target may be achieved in 5 years.
2. Reference Material .... — 10% of allocation
   Normally one book for 20 students.
3. Light material — 5% of allocation
   one book for 50 students
4. Research material .... — 20% of allocation
   one book per 100 student
5. Periodicals — 20% of allocation
6. Classics — 5% of allocation

Total — 100%

Inviting quotations of books is a wasteful exercise. The price printed on the book or given in price list is sufficient. However, the bookseller can be requested to supply photocopy of his suppliers bill.

It will be a good policy if the librarian, on the basis of several factors — reputation of the booksellers their specialisation, (Arts, Science, Commerce, Law, etc.), promptness of delivery, exchange-rates, library discount, other facilities offered, prepares a list of dealers and normally orders are placed with them. This will be beneficial in a number of ways such as replacement of defective books, wrong choice, etc.

The college should avoid the temptation of requesting the big booksellers to display books in the college for 'on the spot' selection of books. In such exhibitions normally those books are brought which are not selling, or are old editions or defective. Teachers are persuaded by the booksellers to select them. Thus, the college is not able to make the best use of its money.

It must be remembered that books which become outdated in foreign countries are available in India at 50 per cent and even more discount. One must be careful while purchasing these books.

With the explosion of knowledge, new and good reference books are coming up in quick succession. No college library can acquire all these books or their latest editions. So, as an alternative, year books, digests, encyclopaedia, etc., should be purchased. This will be economical also.

It is always profitable to place the order of periodicals, Indian as well as foreign, directly with the publisher as:

a) There is dearth of reliable agents.
b) Due to postal vagaries, if some issues get lost, they will never be replaced.
c) The college library can get special discount if the order is placed in the name of the college or a subject teacher.

It will be a good idea to communicate with the Indian Embassies of those countries from where the required journal is published. The Embassy may be persuaded to help the college in procuring the journal and remitting the money to the publishers on behalf of the college.

Local M.P.s and M.L.As be requested to donate the valuable government publications which are supplied to them free of cost and remain dumped with them. Their names be displayed on the Almirahs in which their donations are kept.

The Principal should lay down rules of purchase so that order is placed in a set form after following a set procedure. On receipt of the material, it is checked within a specified time frame for few things, viz., goods supplied are as per order and they are allright. The bills should be forwarded to the account's section within a fixed time. Normally, the payment should go out from the college within one month of the receipt of the material. People should be made accountable for delays.

VII.
CLASSIFICATION AND CATALOGUING SECTION

The Principal should ensure that soon after the newly acquired books arrive, they are classified, numbered and thereafter catalogue cards are prepared. There should be no loss of time. A book loses half its utility if the peak time of the academic session passes out. On an average 75 books should be accessioned per day by one person.

Latest Dewy Decimal classification scheme should be used. Three days are required to catalogue 75 books. All this work should be conducted under the direct supervision of a technical hand, preferably a Deputy Librarian.

VIII.
RESERVED AND PERIODICAL SECTION

Intensive Study Centre

Reserved Section should contain two types of books:

1. Those books which are rare, very popular among readers and the library has only one copy. For example, Dictionaries, Bibliographies, Encyclopaedias, rare and costly subject books, Biographies, Population Census Reports, Parliament or State Legislature Reports, etc., fall in this category.
2. Those text-books which are in great demand and the students want to read them in the library itself. It will be advisable to keep two or three sets of each book in Reserve Section. It is necessary that new text books should be added and old and useless books should be weeded out from this section.

Besides theses books, this section should have all the research journals.

None of these books and periodicals should be issued. A separate catalogue of books and periodicals should be got prepared.

A student should be issued only one book on surrendering his library card, for studying in the Intensive Study Centre. When he returns the book he will get his card back. The author's experience is that this section is very popular amongst students. So, the timings of this section should go on increasing as the examinations approach.

IX.
READING ROOM SECTION

The college should provide a Hall where News-papers are kept on specially made sloppy reading Desks so that readers may come and read them. Reading Room should also have periodicals, magazines, etc.

One class four employee can look after this Reading Room section.

X.
ISSUE, RETURN AND MAINTENANCE SECTION or CIRCULATION SECTION

This section is the most important one and so it should be placed under a Deputy Librarian assisted by able hands.

The Principal should make arrangements that students while entering the library deposit their personal books at the outside counter so that there may be no pilferage of books.

The detailed rules of library use be prepared, printed and given to students. It will be a good idea if after admission, a meeting of new entrants is held and they are given information of how to use the library and what are the essential rules.

The Principal should direct the staff to be very careful about the following things:

1. The books returned by the students should be closely checked for tearing out pages *etc.*
2. The books of which the binding gets loose, worn and torn because of their excessive use are segregated and got repaired.
3. The returned books are stacked the same day at their proper places. Normally due to negligence they are misplaced which later on creates lot of problems. This should not happen otherwise the library will be reduced to a lumber room by the time the examinations draw closer and the students intensify their studies.

   On an average 30 books per hour can be shelved.
4. Reminder should be issued, to students and teachers, if the books are not returned in time. Negligence in this regard often results in a large number of books remaining outstanding in individual names and thereafter it becomes a problem to locate them and get them back. Both, the borrower and the library suffers.

It will be advisable that a system of reserving the books be introduced. It means that a reader can give a slip that he needs such and such books and if they are not immediately available, they should be given to him on priority basis as soon as they are back in the library. In case more than one reader is interested in a particular book, the principle of 'first come, first served' be applied.

The Principal should be specially careful in:

> Getting the library stocks checked on 100 per cent basis soon after the examination starts. The list of lost books be got prepared with all the details.

Certain limited percentage of loss is genuine and it can be accepted but a loss beyond this limit should be the library staff's responsibility. Three per cent loss is admissible, as per Ranganathan. But in other libraries, the practice is to consider loss of .04, or .03 per cent to be normal.

However, this allowance of loss of books to a limited and prefixed extent should apply only to books that remain in general circulation. It cannot apply to Reference Books, or books of the Reserve Section or those which according to Library record, have not been issued. Further, that much of loss should not be taken as a natural right of the library staff. That should be written off only when all hectic efforts to trace the books have failed.

i) Get the damaged books segregated for repairs.
ii) Get the useless books weeded out once a year because they unnecessarily occupy space. Most of the text books are changed from time to time. They should be weeded out. All these books should be sold to the booksellers or donated to sister institutions willing to accept them. Subject teachers should be associated in the weeding process.

The Principal must be very careful in fixing the timings of this Issue-Return section. In the college, if this section functions in lean period, there may be chances of violence and loss of books.

XI.
BOOKS BANK SECTION

The D.S. College, Aligarh was located in a district town but its main clientele was the villages. Bulk of the students belonged to poor families and were probably the first generation of learners. They had no money to purchase books. The author, as a Prof.-in-charge of the

College Library, started a Text Book Loan Scheme on the pattern of the Aligarh Muslim University. Here the students were required to deposit the full value of the book. The entire money deposited was returned, on the spot, when the book was returned after the examination. Detailed rules were made for the scheme. This scheme proved very popular with hardly any loss of books.

The Govt. of U.P. directed the colleges to introduced Book-Bank scheme. A specified portion of Examination Forms Forwarding fees was also diverted for the purpose. Some broad guidelines were also issued. Thus, the scheme got government recognition.

The experience showed:

a) That most of the students prefer not to return the books because by selling the books in the market they got more money than the deposited money. So, there was a huge loss of books.
b) That even those students who returned the books, did it after lot of reminders and efforts. This meant a lot of extra work for the library staff.
c) That the returned books, due to rough use or negligence, or both, needed repairs. The government had not made any provision for rebinding and repairs. The colleges had no spare money to get it done. This meant the books rapidly went out of use.
d) That the sanctioned posts did not warrant deputation of separate staff for this work which continued for the whole year.

It is essential that these difficulties should be overcome with the help of government.

XII.
MISCELLANEOUS SECTION

(Reprography, Audio-visual, Computer and Documentation)

1. *Reprography*

Today readers, specially the Ph.D. students and teachers need pages of books and journals to be photo copied and given to them. Hence, it is essential that the college library may develop Reprographic Section. Today very good Electrostat or X-raying machines are available at reasonable rates from M/s. Canon Plain Paper Copier, New Delhi, Modi X-Rox Ltd., New Delhi, Methodex System P. Ltd., New Delhi, Murphy India Ltd., New Delhi and others. It will be better if that machine is purchased whose spares are easily available and repairing facilities are available locally or at nearby stations. It will be an added advantage if the machine has reduction and enlargement facility.

The reprographic work should be done on market rates. Obviously, other college work can also be handled by this machine when free from the users for whom it is primarily meant.

2. *Audio-Visual Aids*

Today books alone are not considered sufficient to cope with the fast growing pressure of communicating knowledge. So, other aids like the Audio-visual aids are coming up. The most popular are video cassettes and films. So, a college library must try to acquire colour TV Set, Video Cassette players and Video films. Projectors and films may be acquired. A library must appoint a technician to handle these expensive equipment.

3. *Computer*

In the west, computer is increasingly being used in Libraries for the following works:

i) Listing
ii) Accounting
iii) Periodicals control
iv) Books ordering and acquisition
v) Catalogues
vi) Stock verification
vii) Miscellaneous works.

If possible, a college must acquire it and save lot of space and time. This may be profitably used for any number of college works also as preparation of Salary Bill, P.F. Ledger, Students' Ledger, Accounts, etc.

4. *Documentation Centre*

Today a researcher wants a list of published material — books, articles, journals, etc., regarding the topic which be is working on. It is the duty of the college library to provide him such lists. This is known as Documentation service. Many reputed libraries are doing it. For example, Documentation Centre, 36, Feroze Shah Road, New Delhi is rendering this service on payment. The college library must have rapport with these agencies and also start its own service for the benefit of researchers.

XIII.
HEALTH SECTION

(Care and Preservation of Books)

In a library, precious reading material is stocked. Insects and rodents and weather and atmospheric conditions are enemies of the reading material. Hence,

1. Building be so designed (or remodelled) so as to avoid direct sun rays on the books. It must permit fresh air to circulate. It must be made fool proof against water leakage and moisture setting on walls (Relative humidity should not be more than 45°). If need be, the walls be replastered. The mortar should be mixed with damp proof powder. Appropriate precautions should be taken against termite (please refer to Anti-termite treatment in the Chapter on Building). If possible trees and greenery by planted around the library building so that its inside temperature may remain low. Ideal temperature is 22°C -25°C.
2. Vacuum cleaner be provided to the library so that the books and walls are properly dusted off.
3. Rodent like rats and squirrels spoils the books. So, the water drains should be covered with nets, Mouse traps should be fixed at strategic places. Even the rat killing chemicals (Tick -20. etc.) may be used with advantage.
4. DDT powder should be sprayed on walls and racks. Fumes of Tick-20 also kill cockroaches and other insects.
5. Naphthalene and camphor balls should also be used.

6. Floors should be daily swept with Phenyl.
7. Fire extinguishers and water buckets should be installed at various strategic places.
8. Electric wires of special type be used in the library so that the chances of short circuiting are minimum. If possible concealed wiring be got done.
9. If finances permit fumigation chamber and lamination plant should be purchased. They increase the longevity of the documents considerably. The fumigation chamber is available from M/s. W.J. Alcock and Co. P. Ltd. 7, K.S. Roay Road, Calcutta.

Miscellaneous

A Principal must think over these points and take a judicious decision:

1. *Open shelf System:* In the west, most of the libraries have shelf system. It means that the readers are free to move where ever they want and pick up a book or a journal of their choice. This system is good but has lot of practical difficulties in India where that sort of culture among students is still wanting. One is that readers take out books but do not replace them at their proper places. Then the loss of reading material, specially the costly and rare one, is great. No college can afford this luxury at present.
2. *Library Rules and their Publicity:* The Principal should get the detailed rules about every thing prepared. The rules concerning the readers — Book-Bank, Issue system, Reading Room, Reserve Section, *etc.*, be got printed and a copy be given to each student at the time of his admission. It will be a good idea if on the first opening day, an assembly of new entrants is organised and a lecture on *"know thy library"* is given.
3. *Diploma Course in Library Science:* Most of the universities have Diploma Courses in Library Science. It will be a good idea if the college gets permission to start Diploma course. It will enable the college to have extra trained and qualified hands. Besides this, the Diploma students can be used profitably to do different pending works in the library, as a part of their practical training.
4. *Inter-Library Coordination:* Every college is short of funds. So, it cannot purchase all the good literature available. Normally a city has more than one library. So, a scheme of Inter-Library Coor-

dination should be worked out. For example, it may be decided which library will specialise in purchasing research material of what subject. Then they may provide rules for allowing readers of one college to use the other college libraries. Similarly, facilities of providing photo copies be also made available. Inter-Library loaning may also be resorted to. Dozens of such ideas may be given practical form for the optimal use of libraries within their meagre resources.

9

CO-CURRICULAR ACTIVITIES

There is no denying the fact that co-curricular activities—Students' Union, Games, N.C.C. and N.S.S., to name a few—should have an important place in the educational planning since they are to supplement the bookish knowledge and make a student a better man. However, even a cursory look at the style of these activities today will convince anybody that they have not only lost their utility, but most of the present day ills of education are associated with them. Of course, there might be a difference of magnitude from institution to institution or state to state. It is in the fitness of things, therefore, to have a close look at them before taking remedial measures and evolving a comprehensive scheme.

I.
THE STUDENT'S UNIONS

There was a time when Students' Union played a very important role in the life of the student community. They trained students to a democratic way of life. Only meritorious and popular students got elected to different offices of the Union and they managed different associations and functions under the guidance and control of teachers. These functions generated a competitive spirit amongst students and helped them to shine in different spheres—music, dance, drama, debate, poetry, story writing, etc. These student unions also served to bring to the notice of authorities some problems of the students' and seek their redress in a calm and dignified way. It is unfortunate that the student unions which played an important role in pre-independence era have deteriorated and now have become nuclei of all indiscipline, vulgarism and violence. Today the unions' office bearers are elected because of their so called "popularity " which is more with police, with political leaders and other notorious gangs, a factor that sends a chill down the spine of an average student who realises that it is in his own interest to vote for such a "leader".

It is a fact that the union elections are fought almost on the lines of Assembly elections and it is on record that in famous universities, like Delhi, something about rupees one lakh or more is spent by one candidate and the voters are given a royal treatment — free trip to hills, stay in luxurious hotels, best possible food and drinks and every thing just for asking. These elections generate too much heat and sometimes lead to violence on the campus and lead to closure of the academic institutions.

These "popular" leaders organise grand functions, almost at the end of the academic session not with the help of the budding student artists but with the help of mercenaries such as radio artists, noted poets of *Kavi-Sammelan* and *Mushairas,* and all-knowing professional speakers like ministers, politicians and favoured academician-politicians.

These elected office bearers deem it their main duty to keep their own teachers, Principals and Vice-Chancellors "within limits" so that they may not refuse their advice in cases of admissions, attendance, granting of fee concessions, copying in Examination Halls, etc.

These elected leaders are governed and helped in times of need by bosses either of political parties or the under-world, or both.

These students' leaders, who take pride in being called *dadas,* seek admission due to several reasons; Money and power that goes with Student's unions, hunger of leadership, political backing and consequent gains, non-interference by police and so freedom to act freely out-side the institution.

This picture is true at every level of education and in every state; the difference is only of degree.

Chaudhary Charan Singh, observing these developments with concern banned the Students unions in U.P. Smt. Indira Gandhi followed suit during her Emergency Rule. It can be stated that these actions brought peace on campuses. The political parties, in their own interest, could not welcome this peace as it stopped their source of strength. So, in the name of democracy, training the so called future hopes of India and all other flimpsy arguments, the students have once again been restored to their paradise of the Union. So the consequences—breach of peace on campuses — have followed.

The possible benefits of Students' Unions run on healthy lines and the prevailing evils of it force one to think of an alternative. When one can think of controlled democracy, will it be too bad to have controlled unions?

As a Principal, the author made some experiments. They proved beneficial and majority of the students liked them. A Principal can think on similar lines and prepare a scheme of his college, taking into consideration the conditions of the state, the locality and his college.

1. Subject Associations and not Union

The student's unions should be replaced by different subject associations. The membership should be compulsory. There should be no elections. The best students of each class should be nominated to the executive committee of the subject association and the senior most students be appointed as President, Vice-President, Secretary and Joint Secretary. The fees should be minimum and not more than one rupee per student, per year, per subject association. A senior teacher of the subject should be incharge of this association, who should keep a close watch over the activities. Each and every member should attend the meetings and if possible participate also. The meetings should be held once in each month. Besides subject discussions, competitions in music, vocal and instrumental, dance, drama, poetry, debates should be held to select the best. And then in the college annual or closing functions, the competitions among the best of each subject association should be held. Any indiscipline or non-participation should be curbed by disciplinary action.

A Subject Association should concentrate mainly on the activities connected with the subject. It will be better if some field-work is taken up. For example, resource survey of one nearby village per year will be quite rewarding. The results of this survey work should be compiled, debated and suggestions made. A small report should be prepared, copy of which should be available in the library.

2. **Excursions**

Well planned excursions with a view to acquainting students with India, its people and ways of life must be organised, classwise, each year. Going on excursions must be compulsory. During these excursions self reliance should be the key note and wastage should be eliminated. Students should be housed in tents or *Dharmshalas*. Travelling and lodging must be 100 per cent financed by the Government. The tour should not be for less than 10 days and not more than 20 days.

3. Weekly Meet

Principal should hold a fortnightly meeting during the college hours. The membership should be optional. In this meeting Principal and teachers should take up, in a planned manner, topics on morals and religions, how to win friends and influence people, patriotism, etc. Efforts should be made to make the meet most interesting and educative. Audio-visual aids may be utilized. Emphasis should be on illustration from Indian life and conditions.

4. Hobby Workshops

Facility of hobby workshops should be provided where students may prepare themselves to earn while recreating. Some hobby workshops can be:

a) Paintings
b) Commercial paintings
c) Dollmaking which are both educative and remunerative
d) Sculpture
e) Wood work
f) Toy making
g) Leather goods
h) Steno-typing
i) Radio, TV workshop
j) Interior decoration

It is expected that these regulated extra curricular activities will help in developing the personality of students and they will become better socially adjustable. It will give them confidence and develop leadership.

II.
GAMES

Games, outdoor as well as indoor, are as important as Students' Unions because they improve health and change the out look on life by inculcating sportsman-spirit, i.e., smartness, good manners, team spirit, tolerance, competitiveness, etc. In pre-independence period, facilities for games, funds and fields were very limited yet the turn over was good and the standard of games was quite high with no politics vitiating the atmosphere. Today the scene has undergone a drastic change.

The games fees and the number of students in each institution have increased and so the games fund is quite appreciable. In addition to it the U.G.C. has also distributed funds for constructing swimming pools, Gymnasium Halls, etc. Thus there is no dearth of funds. But, on the other hand, the availability of games fields in an institution has remained more of less the same, which, in terms of per capita student, has gone down. Since most of the institutions have slowly become commercial enterprises lacking academic flavour, the shift system has been introduced. Now the importance of an institution lies in number and not quality. So the classes are run from morning till late at night (mainly due to paucity of buildings and furniture). Besides this, most of the students, coming for education, hail from rural areas. Most of the rural students lack the taste of games and as they daily come from neighbouring villages. They are quite tired by the time the class work is over and want to rush back to their sweet homes soon after the classes are over. All this hardly leaves any time and energy amongst bulk of the students to turn up on fields and plunge themselves in different games as ritual.

A casual look at some universities, about half a dozen post graduate colleges having a strength of more than two thousand students, about six intermediate colleges and a few primary schools of U.P. and later, a talk with the Principals and Games incharge revealed that the turn out on the fields is poor, it varies from two per cent to ten per cent (Greater the number, lesser the percentage), regularity and punctually is almost a casualty and consequently the standards of games are at their lowest ebb. This dismal picture becomes more gloomy when one comes to know that bulk of the captains selected or nominated are not necessarily good players of their respective games. They are there with some formidable 'Backing'. Same is true of the players selected to represent the institution. And all this happens (in the name of improving the standards of games) primarily because of the massive games fund and other facilities and the honour that goes with it. For example, each captain is entitled to certain known and unknown privileges such as full fee concession, a dress, power to oblige other players, relaxation in his class attendance and commissions in purchasing games articles, etc.

A Principal cannot easily provide extra playgrounds. Therefore, he should take such steps and form such policies as honest players may be encouraged and pseudo-players may be discouraged.

The Principal should select, amongst the teachers, the players of different games and appoint them as incharges of these games.

The Principal, with the help of these teacher players should frame general rules. These rules should be spelled out:

i) How, from among good and regular players, the captains of the various games will be selected.
ii) What should be the rights and duties of the captains.
iii) What shall be the relationship between Games—Incharges and the captains and players.
iv) How games materials shall be purchased, stocked, issued, etc.
v) The rules of giving dress, shoes, etc., to players be framed.
vi) No extra facilities will be given to captains such as fee exemption, weightage in admission, concession in attendance, etc. Games are a reward in themselves.

Provision of a Games Committee having the representation of students should be made. This games committee must prepare and pass games budged and exercise general control and supervision.

The Principal must ensure that Profs-in-charge of games daily go to the fields and guide and supervise students. If possible, a few more things should be done:

a) Send teams to play friendly matches against good teams of the area. This will generate competitive spirit.
b) Arrange coaching, even for short durations.
c) Send selected players for training at the renowned centres of games.
d) Hold an annual games week and thus open an opportunity for competitions.
e) Award prizes and certificate to the best players of the college in a function.

III.
N.C.C.

Every college has N.C.C. units with its infrastructure of teacher-officers, army officers who are mainly retired, or unfit, or on inactive list, non-commissioned trainers, etc. Crores of rupees are being spent year after year, on this paramilitia so that students may become more disciplined and second line of defence may easily be available in times of need. It is surprising that no serious evaluation has been made of N.C.C. during the past 30 years of its existence. An attempt in the direction is worthwhile.

A visit to the parades show that most of the cadets were not in uniform, i.e., the basic thing for an army training is wanting. The enquiry revealed that the units are short of kits and whatever things are available are not as per size of the cadets. So, the shabby look is unavoidable.

If one may count the heads on the parade and compare them with the list of registered cadets, one will be surprised to note the marked difference between the two. No satisfactory explanation is available except that the style of training is not able to sustain interest amongst the registered cadets and some manipulation, which is in the knowledge and interest of all the concerned, become inevitable.

A look at the parade will disappoint anybody. The cadets are not in a position to march in line and in steps. When this basic training is missing then to think that cadets will be able to handle real rifles, machine guns, etc. is only a far-fetched notion. The reality is that the training with real rifles is habitually not given and the ammunition meant for training is only shown as consumed.

With practically no training imparted, it is not difficult to understand why these N.C.C. trained youngmen generally do not succeed in getting commissions in the army. Even 'B' and 'C' certificate holders have no marking of a soldier in the making.

The most pitiable thing is that most of the army personnel posted in N.C.C. take the job lightly. They have developed a feeling that they are there just to pass time and get a pension. No suggestions are ever demanded from the seniors and when they are given they are not welcomed. The Directorate, like politicians, has also started believing in publicity and playing to galleries. The desire to adopt programmes of adult education will prove it, if a proof is needed.

N.C.C. is a good scheme but an honest effort, planned with imagination, is needed to make it useful at the university level. Here are a few suggestions:

(a) Normally, every university or college has a Proctor and Proctorial Ministry. It should be made a rule that a senior teacher will be the college Proctor and N.C.C. cadets will work as members of the Proctorial Ministry on a rotation basis from amongst the senior cadets. This will automatically end the tension and violence which is associated with the formation of Proctorial Ministry and appointment of Senior Prefects.

b) The Principal through the University and Principals' Association should impress upon the authorities that

i) All the affiliated colleges of a university should be under the command of one Officer Commanding as is the case in Residential Universities.

ii) If the Government has less funds, it should reduce the number of cadets in every college instead of making the training useless.

iii) Every cadet should be provided complete kit, dress, shoes, etc., of his size and that too in time.

iv) The non-commissioned trainers must be from active service and they must be transferred after every three years, to their units. This will make then take their job seriously.

v) Similarly, Commissioned Officers must be from the regular army and they must be transferred after every two years to their units.

vi) Intensive training programme should be planned so that after one session, an N.C.C. cadet, by his look, behaviour, walking, talking, *etc.,* many every inch look like an army man. This training should include use of various fire arms. If college has not a range of its own, the training be organised in some nearby cantonment.

(c) From each college, the best cadets should be selected and they should be given intensive training at some cantonment area so that quite a few of them may be selected for commission.

IV.
N.S.S.

The scheme of N.S.S. was launched with the twin laudable aims. The first aim was to develop a taste for social service amongst our students so that in their later lives they may, as a habit, help their less fortunate brothers and thus continue to contribute to making life more happy. Secondly, the aim was to make our students aware of the realities of life. Unfortunately, this scheme has also gone the way of other schemes.

As far the scheme, a member of N.S.S. is expected to do 120 hours social work in one academic year. The social work comprises teaching children of adults; cleaning premises of the institutions and localities of villages or cities, tree plantation, etc. Besides this 120 hours social work, a ten days camp is also organised which includes all these activities and also briefing by 'experts' on various social problems. This camp is expected to teach community living to the participants. All these activities cannot help in improving matters as they need sustained follow-up action which is missing.

Planning with certain ideas scarcely goes hand in hand with execution. This difference is quite marked in the case of N.S.S. activities. In the first place, the Governments have erred in announcing that an N.S.S. certificate holder will get weightage in admissions to various classes and preference in jobs. Social service is a reward in itself. It should not be treated as an investment. This mentality will defeat the purpose of the scheme, as it has amply done in U.P. Now students enroll themselves for the gains and not for doing honest and sincere work. No wonder then that things are more on paper than in real shape.

Secondly, the consciousness and the habit of doing social service grows slowly. It cannot come all at once. The existing scheme does not envisage of N.S.S., as a daily, continuous, year in and year out programmes. Thus, the very conception is faulty.

Thirdly, it is unfortunate that teachers made incharges of the scheme are not properly selected. They are not given any intensive and well planned training. There are only formal refresher courses, if any. No attempt is made to pool the experiences of a year in an honest way and then remodel the scheme.

All this — defects in the conception of the scheme and defects in its execution — has made the scheme of N.S.S. only a wasteful exercise.

To make N.S.S. useful, certain steps can be taken:

1. N.S.S. incharge should be selected very carefully. Only those teachers, who are sons of the soil in the real sense and who are

known for their moral values and organisational abilities should be picked up.

2. It will be advisable to concentrate on one single village, year after year, instead of hobbing about from one village to another. This will show some results.
3. That village should be picked up from where some students have come to read or some other contact can be established. It will help in developing a confidence which is so very essential to get some good results.
4. A regular rapport must be maintained with the village so that day to day problems of the village are known to the N.S.S. In-charge and he can plan to take steps to help the villagers.
5. It will be ideal to help the villagers in solving their problems. Most of their problems should concern one or the other government department. Because of the college good-will N.S.S. can play a decisive role there. It should act as a liaison agency between the village and the government.

As an illustration a brief narration is ventured below:

i) On the information that sugar-cane crop has caught some disease, students of Botany were sent to know the disease and help the villagers in contending it. The students took time to locate the disease but failed to use the medicine correctly. So, the services of the cane officer were taken. This was of a great educative value for the students and also benefited the villagers.

ii) On the information that malaria has taken an epidemic form, N.S.S. students with a doctor and medicine were sent. It helped the villagers.

iii) A few old and even bachelor youngmen were sterilised during the emergency period. On information, the district administration was requested not to harass the villagers of this N.S.S. village on the condition that the requisite number will be given to them. This made the college a leader of the village.

iv) It was decided that the village lanes will be broadened by demolishing the illegal extension of Platforms. Together with this, *kachcha* drains will be made so that there may not be water logging. Villagers gave a helping hand.

v) Students and teachers of Deptt. of Zoology came out with the brilliant idea that fish breeding and frog breeding ponds should be developed in the village. Villagers were eager. They gave the land but the government department let the college down.

vi) Students and teachers of Botany Department suggested a number of cash crops of medical value or yielding oil to be grown by the villagers. This move also met with partial success.

This is enough to convince that such efforts will be a two way traffic. On one side, students will get a practical knowledge and on the other side, villagers will benefit.

10

HOW TO ORGANISE AND CONDUCT EXAMINATIONS?

In pre-independence days, examinations were fair though in the examination system itself there lurked defects as pointed out by educational experts, particularly those of the U.G.C. Things like leakage of examination papers, mass copying in the examinations and approach to the examiners to get the marks enhanced rampant in the system now were unthinkable. It appears, the more we tried to remove the defects of the examination system — subjective vs. objective, Question Banks, evaluation system, revaluation system, etc., the more we invited new problems. New students, their parents and parents' friends freely indulge in pre-examination, in-examination and post-examination preparations. The "social sense oriented" teacher-politicians think it prudent to help the *"poor"* students. The logic is that even after passing or passing in first division or with first position, it is difficult for a student to get a job. So, why worry and risk life.

The story of practical examination is also not very encouraging. It is a well known fact that the market of group tuitions in science, agriculture and commerce subjects has become lucrative simply because it implies guarantee of good marks in the practicals and also necessary help in theory papers. It is not surprising that the sons and daughters of teacher-leaders are normally position-holders. I have learnt that in some universities, there is no relationship between students' performance in the examination and his marks sheet. On payment of fixed fees any marks sheet — pass, Second Division, First Division or even of above 70 per cent can be secured through the obliging university staff. Aligarh Muslim University has decided to cut down a certain percentage of marks from the official marks sheets of all the universities of a particular state before making the merit of the applicants for admission. In spite of this dictatorial but right decision, the university is not very successful in putting a check on admission of sub-standard students.

The disease of pre-examination, in-examination and post-examination preparations probably started from two States — Bihar and U.P. and is now encompassing the "backward" States. It has almost covered the whole of Northern India.

What a Principal can do under this trying situation ? The best he can think of is to make practical Examination fair, as much as possible, and to minimise, almost finish, use of unfair means of his examination centre. The attempt, of course, involves risk of violence but the Principal must dare and do.

How can these twin objectives be achieved ? Every Principal will have to evolve his own strategy as per the situations prevailing in his college. The author of these lines can only share his experiences.

Practical Examinations

In a meeting of teachers of practical subjects, the following decisions were taken:

1. One coordinator, on the basis of seniority, will be appointed in each Faculty. His work will be to —

   a) Get the names of internal examiners — class-wise and group-wise prepared and send them to the university, to decide who will be the examiner. Uniform rules for all classes will be framed such as seniority-cum-rotation, temporary teachers or those with less than 3 years experience will not be appointed examiner, etc.
   b) Get a time-table of all the practicals of a Faculty prepared. This time-table should ensure that neither laboratories nor staff get over worked or remain free.
   c) As per this time-table, internal examiner should be requested to correspond with the external examiners and request them to stick to the date fixed.
   d) To ensure that the laboratories are prepared for the examinations well in time.
   e) To send the time-table of practicals to the Chief-Proctor of the college with a request that no outsider be permitted near the laboratories where the examinations are on. It

will be the duty of the college Proctor to ensure that examinations are free from any external interference. If need be, he may take help of police force.

f) It should be the duty of the Head of the Deptt. to get the Roll Lists, groupwise, prepared and supply a statement showing divisions and percentage of marks secured by each and every candidate in all the earlier examinations separately in theory and practicals. This statement will give an idea of the students' calibre to the examiners. It should also show the attendance in practicals and the assessment of teachers taking practicals.

g) Not to change the batch of any student under any condition. If a student fails to appear in practical in the batch allotted to him, he is, in no case, allowed to appear in another batch.

h) To ensure that the sealed envelopes of marks are handed over to the Principal before the external examiners leave the station. He should be give.. certificate of having conducted the examination only when he has handed over both the envelopes one for the university and another for the college.

2. Practical Examinations are a team work. So, the internal-examiner should be free to select any colleague to assist him. Besides this, it will be the duty of the Head of the Deptt. to depute a senior teacher of the department also. He will be available during the entire duration of the examination, in the department. He will also keep a vigil.
3. When the results are out and marks of the students have been received by the college, the Principal should hold departmental meetings to analyse the results. Special notice should be taken of those cases where the difference in theory and practicals is marked or the marks of practicals do not compare well with the marks in earlier examination, or the assessment of teachers taking practicals in the whole session differs widely with the actual marks received. These discussions should also take note, if less marks are given to a candidate. These in-depth discussions, expose the erring ones. None wants to be exposed.

This exercise makes it obligatory that the practicals start in the college at the right time and are conducted seriously throughout the session.

Theory Examinations

To make Theory Examinations clean the following steps proved very effective:

1. An Examination Office was set up. The very best amongst the senior most teachers and non-teachers were selected for this office. One will have to accept the fact that even today people appointed prior to 1960 are more sincere, more hard working and integrity oriented. Of course, some youngers, who are to be trained up, will have also to be picked up. This office should be the eye, the ear and the hand of the Principal.

   The Examination Office should ensure that the examination work runs strictly as per Examination Rules and Regulations. Special attention should be paid to the following:

   a) A teacher should be appointed as incharge of answer books. He should maintain a record of answer books, classwise. Daily checking of balances be done.
   b) As far as possible, not less than two teachers should be kept as invigilators in one room. It means that biggest rooms be selected for holding examinations.
   c) The roomwise placement of teachers should be done very carefully. No room should be left with a weak team of Invigilators. Every room must have at least one senior and one tough teacher. The junior or weak ones be associated with the seniors or toughs but be not given independent charge of any examination room. This duty chart ensures 50 per cent clean examination.
   d) Seating Plan, of each room be made and examinees must be made to sit on the allotted seats. This seating plan should be put up on Notice-Board just half on hour before the commencement of the examination.

Rooms of each candidate should be changed in every examination paper.

Room seating plan along with Examination Forms should be sent to each room within 10-15 minutes of the commencement of the examination so that the invigilator may check up the students Roll Numbers with the Seating Plans and also their signatures and faces with the signatures and photos on the Examination Form.

It is desirable to have seating done in a compact area so that in time of need all the invigilators and members of the flying squad can work effectively.

To prepare detailed instruction for the Invigilators and provide a copy to all the teachers.

To place watermen outside the Examination rooms so that water can be supplied inside the rooms. This will facilitate examinees and also prevent chances of getting material from outside. Similarly, improvised urinals should also be errected in close vicinity of the different examination wings. Care should be taken to keep these urinals clean and free from odour.

To collect the answer-books, pack them and send them to the examiners/university daily and keep a record. It will be ideal if Code Number is given on Railway P.W. Bill and packet and bundles of different classes and papers are mingled in such a way that it may become impossible for the Railway Staff or College Staff to know where the answer books are being sent.

An Internal Flying Squad should be organised. The Proctor and about a dozen trusted teachers, both young, strong and senior should form this squad. It's work should be:

i) To search and remove the papers, books and other copying material from classrooms, verandahs, toilets and other hiding places.

ii) To close all entrance gates except one and there to allow students to enter the college after checking identity cards and Roll Numbers. No outsiders should be allowed inside the college.This checking must start after getting the campus cleaned from students and at least 30 mts. before the commencement of examination. If the entrance points are more, to have checking at every entrance point.

iii) To put police at strategic points so that it may be immediately available on need.

iv) To close gates and bar entry without permission after the paper has been distributed. This work be entrusted to police.

v) Check examinees after 30 minutes of starting of papers. Desk, tables and person of students be checked thoroughly after giving warning. Special attention should be paid to writings on the desks and walls. It is essential that the desks be rubbed and cleaned with wet cloth daily.

vi) to be vigilant and take rounds of the Examination Halls regularly. It will be better if Flying Squad is divided into groups and posted in different areas.

vii) Room walls should also be checked closely. Any thing written thereon should be got rubbed.

The Principal should approach the university to treat members of the Flying Squad as on duty and make payments to them.

viii) The Notice Boards of each room should be daily cleaned and rubbed with cloth.

3. (a) Cases of unfair means should be reported indiscriminately but not recklessly. Recklessness makes the teachers, in the eyes of the examinees, an assortment of freaks and enemies and not fair guard and guardians of examination system and, in turn, rouses tendency of revolt. This then enjoins that teachers should not exercise physical force and should not treat the examinees with blore as the young among the teachers are generally prone to do. Every such case should be processed according to statutory provisions and with the paper formalities. Of course, if a student tends to be violent, mild force may be exercised to overpower him and the rest should be left to the police. It is the dignity of the teachers and not the muscle power that creates awe among students.

(b) Answer books and allied papers relating to cases of unfair means should be packed, sealed and despatched to the university promptly so that pressure may not mount to save them and awkward situations may be avoided.

(c) The report of the Invigilator, Superintend Examination and Principal should not be vague or in general terms. It must be specific and honest. Most of the cases had to be let out by the University because the reports were not properly written.

4. Other Precautions

The pre requisites of a clean examination are:

i) No bad student with a criminal record be admitted. And if one is admitted, he must be persuaded or forced to leave the college.

ii) The teaching must be regular and intensive. The Principal should ensure that the courses are completed well in time. If need be, extra classes be takcn. This should be done by creating an atmosphere of belonging to the college.

iii) Insistance on attendance should be there. After every month, the parents of the students having less than 50-60 per cent attendance be informed. In no case, students with less than 60 per cent attendance be allowed to appear at the examination. And this is possible only when monthly information is sent to the parents and concerned students are also informed. It will be a better idea if cards of different colours are got printed for informing parents.

11

COLLEGE DEVELOPMENT AND FUNDING AGENCIES

A Principal should realise that most of the Private Managements do not collect funds for the college and normally, the State Government has also not much funds to spare. So, a Principal should know the sources from where he can secure funds for the maintenance of the excellence of the college, its development and providing funds to teachers for their academic pursuits. A brief narration of a few agencies from where funds can be secured are mentioned below:

I.
UNIVERSITY GRANTS COMMISSION
(Bahadur Shah Zafar Marg, New Delhi)

Today education is in the concurrent list. So, it is the responsibility both of the State Government and the Central Government to look to the planned expansion of Higher Education and also maintenance of its academic excellence. With this end in view, the Central Government established the U.G.C. in 1956.

The aim of he U.G.C. is to provide and coordinate higher education, to determine and maintain standards of teaching, examinations and research in the universities, both Residential and Affiliating. It has the authority to assess the financial needs of the universities and colleges and to give appropriate grants. It advises the Central Govt. on the establishment of new universities and other matters pertaining to higher education. It has, however, nothing to to do with the expansion of higher education or with the Primary or Secondary Education.

A convention of teachers of the Agra University was held in the sixties in which following points were raised:

1. Expenditure on education should be treated as investment.

This is the most important investment because it deals with human capital.

2. Eighty per cent of higher education is provided by the affiliating colleges at the door step of students, most of whom are first generation of learners. The U.G.C. gives only 10 per cent of its funds to colleges and 90 per cent to Central and State Universities. This is neither logical, nor democratic nor socialistic. The policy should be made more rational.
3. These 10 per cent of funds which are given to the colleges are for non-essential items like swimming pools and not for the priority sector.

The U.G.C., thereupon, appointed a committee under the Chairmanship of Shri V.S. Jha to go into these details and make recommendations. The committee visited all the University headquarters of the affiliating universities and talked mainly with the Vice-Chancellors, Registrars, Deans, etc., who had not much knowledge of facts. This committee also visited Aligarh and met, per chance, the Principals of local colleges of the Agra University. There the committee was provided a lot of information and ideas. The net result was that the funding policy of the U.G.C. underwent a sea change.

The position as it stands today can be presented in a tabular form (Table 11.1).

Table 11.1 reveals some important and interesting facts:

1. During the past 20 years, as per U.G.C. report, percentage increase in students' enrolment per year,has been continuously falling. In 1969-70, increase over the preceding year was of 2.26 lakh students, i.e., 14.5 per cent. As compared to it in 1988-89, increase over the preceding year was of 1.33 lakh students, i.e. 3.5 per cent.
2. In 1988-89, out of 39.47 lakh students, 32.93 lakh students were reading in colleges, i.e., 83.4 per cent and only 6.54 lakh students, i.e., 16.6 per cent were in the Central Universities, Deemed Universities and State Universities. Yet it appears, that the college sector is a neglected sector. U.G.C. gives then only plan grants and the State Governments provide them maintenance grants which are quite poor. This is borne out by several parameters.

TABLE 11.1: Some Important Data

Sl. No.	Description	1950-51	1988-89
1.	Central Universities	27	144
2.	Deemed Universities	—	27
3.	Colleges	542	6,912
4.	*Students' Enrolment*		
	a) Universities	N.A.	6.54 lakhs
	b) Colleges	N.A.	32.93 lakhs
	c) Total	3.6 lakhs	39.47 lakhs
5.	*Teachers*		
	a) Universities	N.A.	54,973
	b) Colleges	N.A.	1,94,095
	c) Total	18,648	2,49,068
6.	*Grants (Plan)* (Given by UGC)		
	a) Central Universities	N.A.	28.45 Crores
	b) Deemed Universities	N.A.	12.95 Crores
	c) State Universities	N.A.	99.99 Crores
	d) Colleges	N.A.	44.04 Crores
	e) Total	N.A.	185.43 Crores
7.	*Grants (Maintenance)* (Given by U.G.C.)		
	a) Central Universities	—	8414.60 Crores
	b) Deemed Universities	—	1954.03 Crores
8.	*Average No. of Students* (1988-89)		
	a) Colleges		476.41
	b) Universities		3824.56
	c) Total		557.24
9.	*Teacher-Student Ratio* (1988-89)		
	a) Colleges		1:16
	b) Universities		1:11
	c) Total		1:15
10.	*Grants per student plan* (1988-89)		
	a) Colleges		Rs. 137 per student
	b) Universities		Rs. 690 per student
	c) Total		Rs. 475 per student

3. Teacher-student ratio in colleges which cater to 83 per cent of higher education is 1:16. Obviously, in compulsory subjects at under-graduate level it must be quite bad. On the other hand,

ii) *College Science Improvement Programme (COSIP)* — It aims at creating scientific temper amongst students and teachers. A college can get Rs. one lakh per year for three years. This scheme is for under-graduate students.

iii) *Restructuring of Under-graduate Courses* — A college can avail itself of a grant of Rs. 1 lakh per year for a period of 5 years. The whole idea is to introduce new subjects and allow non-traditional combinations of subjects. U.G.C. has prepared a list of such subjects. Of course, a college, by itself, cannot do it.

iv) *Autonomous College* — Out of 6912 colleges, 95 colleges, i.e., 1.3 per cent colleges have been granted the status of an Autonomous college by the U.G.C. An autonomous college becomes almost a mini-university with full freedom to decide the course contents of subjects, to restructure combination of subjects, to hold examinations, etc. The idea behind this is to make them like Community Colleges of U.S.A. where efforts are made to meet the cultural and developmental needs of the locality. The U.G.C. gives liberal grants to these colleges. The U.G.C. has recently introduced the scheme of *Autonomous Departments.*

v) *Computer Facilities* — This is a new scheme. Under it, computers are provided to the colleges.

vi) *National Adult Education Programmes and Jan Shikshan Nilayams* — 1278 colleges have been sanctioned Adult Education Centres and 889 Jan Shikshan Nilayams. They have been given financial assistance.

vii) *Planning Forums* — The commission provides assistance to colleges for the establishment of Planning Forums @ Rs. 5000 p.a. per institution.

viii) *U.G.C. Film Study Centres* — A college can apply, subject to fulfilling the U.G.C. norms, for U.G.C. Film Study Centre. A Centre at Pune has been established to ensure supply of suitable films, equipment, etc.

ix) *Improvement of Sports and Games Facilities*

x) *Remedial Coaching Classes* — Colleges can be given substantial assistance up to Rs. 4 lakhs for organising remedial coaching classes for students belonging to weaker sections of the society, specially the scheduled castes and scheduled tribes.

xi) *University Leadership Project (U.L.P.)* — With a view to improving the quality of teaching in colleges in selected subjects, the affiliating university is given this project, departmentwise. This university Deptt. acts as a guide and philosopher for the subject in the affiliated colleges.

5.Faculty Improvement Programme

With a view to improving quality of teachers, the following schemes have been floated by the U.G.C.:

a) *Teacher Fellowship for M.Phil* — Under this scheme, a teacher will get one year leave with pay for his M.Phil degree. For every five permanent teachers, one fellowship to the maximum of eight can be sanctioned in one year. The essentials to get this fellowship are: age less than 45 years, a minimum of three years service and atleast 50 per cent marks in Post-graduate examination.

b) *Participation in International Conferences Abroad* — A college teacher can be sanctioned financial aid to attend an international conference abroad if his paper has been accepted. A teacher will be eligible for assistance only once in three years. Fifty per cent expenses are paid by the U.G.C.

c) *Participation in Refresher Courses, Workshops, Seminars, Symposia, etc.*

d) *Support for Research* — In-service teachers are given financial assistance for Minor Projects (Maximum of Rs. 15,000,00) and Major Projects (No limit of money).

e) *Grants for writing Text Books*.

f) *National Fellowships* — Thirty national fellowships are available for teachers so that they may get one year leave with full pay to devote themselves whole heartedly to research. They will be paid extra Fellowship allowance of Rs. 500 p.m. plus a non-lapseable grant of Rs. 5000.

g) *National Associateship* — Under this scheme one teacher gets leave with pay for one year, three years, on five years. The number of associateships is 100.

6. Miscellaneous

The U.G.C. has done several good things with a view to raising the quality of education. Some of these things are:

i) *National Information Centres* — These centres are located at Bangalore, Bombay and Baroda. One can get oneself registered there and get informations in the computerised forms.

ii) *University Science Instrumentation Centre* (U.S.I.C.) *and Regional Instrumentation Centre* (R.I.C.) — To repair and service instruments, design and fabricate attachments to the existing requirement and to train instrument scientists and technicians, the U.G.C. has approved proposals of 57 universities for setting up U.S.I.Cs. Besides this, Indian Institute of Sciences, Bangalore and Western Regional Instrumentation Centre, Bombay University have also been approved.

iii) *Publications of Results and Awards in Science Education Journals.* They are published quarterly in Physics, Mathematics, Biology and Chemistry. They are given free of cost on demand. Besides these journals, grants to Universities for Publication of learned/research work is also given.

iv) *Centenary Grants and Jubilee Grants* — Colleges are given block grants to commemorate their centenary and Jubilee years as under:

a) Completion of 25 years	up to 5 lakhs
b) Completion of 50 years	up to 20 lakhs
c) Completion of 100 years	up to 25 lakhs

7. Follow up Action

To apply in time to get funds is one thing and to ensure their proper utilisation and completion of formalities like sending Audited Accounts and Progress Reports is another. So, a Principal should be very very careful in this regard.

It is advisable that he should entrust the duty of maintaining U.G.C. accounts to an account's clerk. Further, a Ledger Register should be introduced in which the Funds sanctioned for different items be mentioned with expenses incurred. The posting should be up to date. A column should be added to indicate the details of orders placed and advances given. This register should be seen by the Principal at regular intervals as it will give him an idea of what has been done and what more is to be done. It will help in disciplining the work.

The Principal should entrust some one to maintain constant contact with the Director, College Development Council of his University and also the U.G.C. office at New Delhi for finding out new schemes, new norms and getting application forms, etc., well in time.

II.
INDIAN COUNCIL OF SOCIAL SCIENCE RESEARCH
(35, Ferozeshah Road, New Delhi-110001)

The Indian Council of Social Science Research (ICSSR) has a programme of supporting the research of individual Social Scientists by offering research fellowships at various levels. The discipline recognised for such support are Economics, Commerce, Education, Business Management, Psychology, Political Science, Sociology, Social work, etc., and the Social Science aspects of Anthropology, Demography, Geography, History, Law and Linguistics.

The objectives of the programmes are:

1. To provide opportunities to social scientists to engage themselves, on a whole time basis, in important research work in which they are currently interested;
2. To provide facilities to social scientists to write books;
3. To assist young social scientists, who have shown sufficient promise and competence for research work of merit to work on full time basis on their approved proposals of research.

ICSSR awards following research fellowships:

i) *National Fellowship* — Council offers these Fellowships on its own initiative. The number of such fellows is nine.

ii) *Senior Fellowship* — These are sanctioned primarily to professional social scientists on the applications received. The are of 2 years' duration. The age limit is 65 years. They are paid salary which they were drawing at the time of retirement or Rs. 3,000 p.m.

iii) *General Fellowship* — These are sanctioned on the applications received. They are of 2 years' duration. They are meant for young social scientists who have completed their Ph.D. Superannuated and retired scholars are not eligible. Employee scholars will be given salary protection and allowances admissible at the parent institution of the scholar. To those not employed, a consolidated fellowship of Rs. 2,500 per month will be given. Further, they will be paid a contingency grant of Rs. 7,500 per annum.

III.
COUNCIL OF SCIENTIFIC AND INDUSTRIAL RESEARCH

The Council of Scientific and Industrial Research (C.S.I.R.) Complex, Pusa, New Delhi provides financial assistance to promote research in the fields of science and technology. Any science teacher of a post-graduate department can apply for the grant.

A project is submitted to the C.S.I.R. which gets it screened before sanctioning the amount.

There is no limit of the amount to be sanctioned.

A research investigator, if he likes and on the basis of the magnitude and nature of the scheme submitted, may have paid Junior Research Fellows (J.R.Fs) or Senior Research Fellows (S.R.F.s). The Ph.D. students of the investigator or of colleagues may be appointed.

The C.S.I.R. sanctions contingent and equipment grants also. Contingent grants can be utilised for tours and purchase of books and journals. The equipment grant is for purchase or fabrication of a particular equipment essential for the project.

C.S.I.R. permits the college to retain books, journals and equipment purchased for the project out of the C.S.I.R. funds.

Thus, C.S.I.R. helps teachers in doing good research work and enables the department to get rare books, journals and equipment which it could otherwise not get with its own resources. It also helps Ph.D. students to earn while learning.

The Principal may depute a person to maintain close contact with the C.S.I.R. office to know of the new schemes, new norms and get application forms.

IV.
DEPARTMENT OF SCIENCE AND TECHNOLOGY

Department of Science and Technology (D.S.T.), Technology Bhawan, New Mehrauli Road, New Delhi, in collaboration with the Planning Commission decided to help young scientists. So, a scheme has been initiated to provide financial support for seminars/symposia, research projects, travel within and out side the country and for publications. Special encouragement is given to the young scientists below the age of 35 years.

Young scientists award are also given for scientific contributions. These awards are given through Indian National Science Academy, Bahadur Shah Zafar Marg, New Delhi and Indian Science Congress Association, 14, Dr. Biresh Guha Street, Calcutta.

The Principal should entrust some one to collect the latest information, application forms, etc., from the D.S.T. office, New Delhi.

V.
DEPARTMENT OF ENVIRONMENT

Department of Environment, Forests and Wild-life, C.G.O. Complex, Lodhi Road, New Delhi, is relatively a new department. The environment management is connected with overall ecological, cultural, economic, social, technological and other factors. So, it requires collection of baseline data and background data. After acquiring the idea of the quality of environment, the second phase is to know how changes in this quality will effect various aspects of man-health, property, aesthetic values, etc. Lastly after identifying physical effects, efforts must be made to know how to control them and improve environment. Thus, the studies cover a wide range of subjects and aspects.

The Department of Environment sanctions projects to the college teachers of various disciplines ın specific identified areas. The project covers (i) appointment of research associates/fellows and technical supporting staff on payment of salaries, etc. (ii) acquisition of equipment, (including computer), (iii) Travel grants, (iv) contingency grants for books, journals, etc.

All equipments and stores purchased out of the grant would remain with the institution concerned.

12

THE HOSTELS

At present very little attention is being paid to college hostels and practically no philosophy has been developed concerning them. Today, very little hostel facilities are available at colleges and wherever they exist, they are not adequate and conducive to a proper atmosphere of studies and personality development of the inmates. Buildings are in dilapidated conditions. Toilets and bath-rooms are at a long distance from living rooms, Dining rooms are non-existent and kitchens are in horrible unhygienic conditions. Students are stuffed in a room to its maximum capacity. There is hardly any furniture, beds, almirahs, ceiling fans and other essentials. And worst, there is a hostel warden in name. There is no supervision and control not to say of personal rapport between hostelers and hostel warden.

Today, hostels have become dens of vulgarism, indiscipline and sources of major problems of the educational institutions. Instances are not wanting when outsiders and undesirable elements reside in hostels with immunity as these places are considered out of bounds for police. Collection of unlicensed arms and, on occasions, their free use, is not an exception. Hostel life becomes a terror for good inmates who, sooner than later, are forced either or quit or fall in line. The rural folks, lacking educational background and parental control, soon get enamoured of this life and provide teeth and muscles. On the whole, the atmosphere is anti-social and certainly not conducive for studies, character building and higher things of life.

It is a matter of common knowledge that the hostelers can be grouped, on the basis of indiscipline and misbehaviour, in the following order — technical and professional students (Engineering, M.B.B.S and Teachers education), Commerce, Arts, Science and Law students.

Should Hostels be Wound Up?

Here a pertinent question arises. When we have failed to insulate students from bad elements and provide a healthy atmosphere in hostels, what is the use of maintaining them. Why should they not be wound up? In that case at least they will cease to be a source of headache to the institution. The answer, in the existing context, will be a 'YES'. However, in the new context, which we propose to plan, hostels can be made to play a very vital role and can be light houses.

A peep in lumber rooms of Nalanda and Taxila will show that most of the magnificent achievements attributed to these ancient seats of learning were the result of their hostels. It is also a known fact that in ancient India residence was a prerequisite in *Gurukuls*. Even in the famous universities of the world today, the hostels are playing a key role. And the rationale is not difficult to understand. For bearing a stamp and building a specified character, students need to be isolated from unhealthy influences, attractions and deteractions and given individualistic care and guidance in a friendly way in a controlled atmosphere. All this is possible only through hostel life.

Where the Fault Lies?

In modern India, hostels are the legacy of British days. They have grown in present India not according to any planned and predetermined objectives. The U.G.C., the State Governments and other charitable institutions and individuals, both Indian and Foreign, had the money bags, which they never knew where to throw. Like swimming pools, hostels became a fad and mark of respectability. Today, a situation has arisen where hostel buildings are there without enough residents or where buildings are insufficient to cope with the demand. And worst of all, the hostel accommodation has no relationship with the need, aspirations and character of the educational institution. For example, in a college or even a university, where predominantly students come from rural areas, posh modern architectures, full with modern facilities, are provided and, believe it or not, the result within a year, is that most of these modern amenities like equipment in dinning halls, bath rooms and toilets get damaged and even the electric installations are not spared. Is it not surprising that the hostels have, by and large, no library, no games facilities and no healthful activities. Not only this. Students are not screened before being given a seat in a hostel probably because none has an idea of what type of atmosphere will be built in the hostel and for that atmosphere what type of boys are desirable. Every one knows how much effort and sacrifice is done by parents and how much pains under gone before their sons and daughters become worth something. Is it not shocking that no assessment is made of the willingness and capabilities of a teacher before selecting him as a Provost or a Hostel Warden? Today these posts have become seats of patronage devoid of any corresponding sense of duty and ability. The wardens do not even recognise students, who are put under their charge. How can, then, they be expected to know their physical, psychological, academic and social problems and help them in solving them. The relationship which should have been of a father and a son has deteriorated into one of an officer and a subordinate. It is this absence of love, sincerity and direction coupled with indifference towards responsibilities and even increasing self-interest of keepers of hostels that today hostels and hostelers have become a blot and a disgrace.

In the name of emotional integration, secularism, casteless and creedless society, new experiments are being made without ever bothering to evaluate the results or preparing the ground. For example, at the Aligarh Muslim University, in the name of emotional integration, not only in each Hall and Hostel, but even in rooms non-Muslims were housed with Muslims. This might have given good results, had efforts been made to bring both of them closer by changing their ways of life, thinking and acting. This was not done. So, in the absence of mutual understanding and spirit of give and take, psychological tensions started mounting up. Muslim students thought that it is their university and therefore they are superior and controller of the situation. The non-Muslims, while accepting the reality, refused to adjust themselves and tried to maintain a separate identity. The very purpose of the scheme became the first casualty and, in trail, generated psychological problems. The same is true of housing students of different castes in the same hostel and in the same room. In place of homogeneity and good relations new problems crop up and the whole atmosphere gets vitiated. The new idea of mixing scheduled caste students with others, without making the necessary background, may prove to be more disastrous than useful.

The Purposes

The aims and object of establishing and running a hostel by an educational institution should be:

(i) *To Provide Cheap and Workable Accommodation*

It is natural that in some educational institutions students may seek admission from far and nearby places-neighbouring villages, cities, or even from outside the state. The number of such students will depend upon the reputation of the institution and the classes and the courses it is running. Normally, at primary level or even at high school and secondary stage the number of such students will be microscopic provided the institution has not built up a reputation for itself like some Public Schools. In technical and professional courses also, where the seats are very limited, the competition for admissions is likely to be at all India level. In such institution where students come from outside, hostels become a must as they provide cheap and correct type of boarding and lodging facilities to students.

Cheapness and luxury do not go together. Hence, hostels should have workable buildings and equipment and no ornamentation or luxury should be permissible. Further, too many comforts and luxuries are enemies of character. Good foundations for building character can be laid down only when the living conditions are just comfortable enough for proper living and studies, but are not lavish. Simplicity and dignity should be the guiding criteria.

(ii) *To Provide an Atmosphere which may Supplement the Efforts of an Educational Institution*

As mentioned earlier, the aim and object of an educational institution is to help a student in an all-round integrated development. Hostels should supplement and assist in fulfilling this goal, by providing suitable facilities and environment for

1) Physical development
2) Intellectual development
3) Moral development
4) Spiritual development
5) Love for the country and the world.

A student is likely to stay for some hours in the educational institution but the rest of the day, he is expected to spend in hostel. So to wean the hostelers from the evil forces and help them in their all round development is the most important task of the hostel.

(iii) *To Teach Good Manners, Social Awareness and Organising Techniques*

Hostel life will be reduced to a misery if hostelers do not display good manners, social adjustments, spirit of give and take and willingness to assist in the management of their kitchen, hostel administration, etc.

The Programme

The translate these aims and objects into action the following programme can be ventured:

1. The hostel buildings should be constructed at the outskirts of the town as the land will be cheaper and chances of distraction will be minimum. The building should not be ornamental but cheap and durable.
2. Efforts should be made to provide all the necessary facilities conductive to healthy living but no excessive comforts or luxuries should be provided.
3. Self-help should be the motto, hence, minimum number of servants should be engaged. No individual services to students should be permitted. Cleanliness should be of a high order. If need be, a day in a month fixed for mass cleaning campaign by students themselves.
4. It should be compulsory for students to participate in the morning P.T. Those who are interested in gymnasium, athletics or *yoga* may be exempted.
5. Food must be rich and balanced but simple. It will not be a bad idea if dishes of different States are served from time to time.
6. It will be better if a working library is attached with the hostel which may meet the need of hostelers for both classroom work and general knowledge. Collection of autobiographies, religious works, useful books like 'How to influence People and Win Friends' should be in the hostel library. A record should be kept of every hosteler showing the duration of studies and the books consulted. If need be guidance should be given by the Warden, or other attached teachers.
7. Efforts must be made to know the weak spots in studies of

hostelers. These weak spots should be removed with the help of senior students of the hostel and if need be with the assistance of subject teachers of the college.

8. Extra Co-curricular activities like debate, lectures, symposia, group discussions, etc., should be organised on topics not directly connected with the class -room studies. It will be better if short courses on moral preaching, social awareness, patriotism, music, both vocal and instrumental, painting, sculpture, etc., are organised and each and every hosteler is persuaded to join them according to his taste and liking. It is essential to keep records and make evaluations at short durations and, if need be, to introduce changes. These activities must be organised daily only in the afternoons for one hour.
9. Short study tours to religious, historical, educative places and picnic spots be organised in which participation should be compulsory.
10. Ample recreation facilities should be available in the hostel. But these facilities should be available only in the evening for fixed duration.
11. Rules of hostel life should be made and enforced strictly. These rules should be revised from time to time in consultation with students.
12. Students participation in each and every activity should be *sine qua non*.

The Pitfalls

The success or failure of a hostel depends on two factors—the hostel warden and the inmates. If a right teacher with a missionary zeal and vision is entrusted with this herculian task, then half the battle will be won automatically. The other prerequisite is to select the inmates carefully. If, under a wrong assessment, a few depraved type of students are admitted and if they are not quickly turned out, then the whole thing will end into a chaos.

It will be a good idea if some sincere and disciplined teachers are also attached with the hostel. They should divide hostlers among themselves and act as their guardians.

The U.G.C.

The U.G.C. does not give grant to colleges for hostels. It will be ideal if U.G.C. can think of funding the college hostels for the following purposes:

1. Constructing of new buildings or modifying the existing ones.
2. Providing necessary facilities — Hostel library, indoor games, remedial coaching classes, coaching classes for competitive examinations, study tours, canteen, *etc.*
3. Substantial allowance to teachers, associated with hostels.

13

POINTS TO PONDER OVER

Principal is the pivot of the academic life of an institution. As such, he is a Manager and an Administrator which also means a leader and a motivator. It will be worthwhile to understand clearly the meaning of these high sounding words.

I.
A MANAGER

The functions of management are to be differentiated from the functions of an administrator. None doubts that President F.D. Roosevelt was a great administrator though it is a point of dispute whether he was a great President or a national disaster.

A good management

1. *fixes goals and sub-goals to be achieved in set periods of time.* In case of an academic institution, the ultimate goal can be to make the institution an elite one by producing an all round integrated and balanced developed end-products. How much of this ultimate goal will be achieved at the end of each academic session will be the sub-goals. Here students will be just like raw materials which are to be converted into finished products with the help of teachers (human capital) and infrastructure — non-teachers, library, laboratories, buildings, office, games facilities, finances, etc.
2. *decides how this ultimate goal and sub-goals are to be achieved.* In case of an industry, a manager decides in which proportions the various factors of production are to be combined so that optimal results are achieved, i.e., maximum good quality production is achieved at the cheapest cost. He decides whether it will be profitable to have more of labour or more of

capital ? Similarly, the manager of an academic institution will have to decide what combination of teaching hours, laboratory work, library work, extra-curricular activities, games, physical exercise, moral orientation, etc., will help in an all-round integrated and balanced development of students. The manager of the institution will decide the proportions of various inputs so that students optimal development may take place as per their genes, natural faculties and capacities.

3. *helps in going up and staying at optimal point.* Once the goal is achieved, the question will be how to sustain it. Normally, after the maximum is achieved every one feels complacent and so starts relaxing and becomes inactive. Thus, a trend towards downfall necessarily starts. The manger should device ways and means to keep things in stream line so that quality of end-products may remain at optimum point. If necessary, the proportions, etc. of inputs may also be altered or modified.

In short, the functions of a manager is to manage the academic institution, to manage the managers and to manage workers and work. And all this management should be on the basis of time-element. In case of management of an academic institution, three time-elements become important, *viz.*, present (the starting point), future (the ultimate aim) and in between (at time intervals) say one academic session, to evaluate and plan for future.

Short- and long-term planning is essential for the development of an educational institutions. Before starting planning one will have to take care of four letters — SWOT.

S — Strength :	List the strong points which could be management, solid traditions, discipline, faculty, physical facilities, Unions, *etc.*
W — Weakness :	All the above or a few of them could be weaknesses. List them.
O — Opportunities:	Political, social traditions, U.G.C., University, Government and so on.
T — Threats:	They are external, some are beyond control, namely, spurt of communal riots. Many could be titled in opportunities.

Planning should be in connection with (1) academic, (2) physical,

(3) extra-curricular, (4) campus, etc.

The Principal should prepare organisational and functional plan and then execute it. It may be remembered that "Rome was not built in a day." In long-term planning, tenure and SWOT should be cautiously taken into account.

By and large a Principal is the internal manager of the college. It is he who manages the academic side, the college office and its financial resources, expenditure, physical facilities, human resources, etc. In the management of the affairs he will face

a) Conceptual problems
b) Legal problems
c) Organizational problems
d) Procedural and functional deficiencies
e) Information problems
f) Problems in human relations
g) Problem of hardware, and
h) Personnel problems.

Academic Side — Awareness of recent developments.
— Academic aptitudes of individual teachers.
— Best students assessed on the basis of their studies and personal contact with them.
— Encouragement for research.
— Regular classes for maximum number of days.
— Periodical review of progress of teaching, analysis and fixing of targets.
— Evaluation technique, evaluation and review.
— Self Assessment of teachers and Principal, its review.

In India, academic institutions are either government owned, in which case government becomes the manager; or private owned, in which case private trusts become managers; or societies owned, in which case private managing committees become managers. In all the three cases, the Principal is necessarily associated as an ex-officio member of the Management. So, he has always a key role to play. It is another thing that a Principal may himself be ignorant of the functions which he should perform as a member of the Managing Committee, or he should consider it wise to be a silent spectator and an yielding figure in self-interest.

It is generally observed that the members of the Managing Committees (or Board of Trustees), are themselves ignorant of the functions which they should perform viz., fix goals and sub-goals, provide infrastructure and lay down guidelines to combine various inputs, at time intervals, to achieve goals and stick there. In the absence of this knowledge, naturally they are misled to think that their role is of an administrator and not of a policy-maker. This misunderstanding or intentional tresspassing into the sphere of an administrator, often leads to encouragement of teacher politics and clashes with the Principal. Consequently, the progress of the institution suffers.

It has been generally observed that even the State Governments are not clear about the functions and the utility, of the Managing Committees. So, they have failed to take a decision about the nationalisation of Private Managements and Private Trusts. This is more peculiar when they have taken away from the Managements, various responsibilities such as provide infrastructure, to find money for salaries, for books and magazines, for laboratories, equipments, for construction of buildings, etc. Even the right to appointment and punish has been more or less taken away from them.

Under these conditions, it appears, the managements functions is with none — Principal, Managing Committees, University, Government, University Grants Commission or Central Government. Every one is trying to have a partial say with no responsibility or accountability. The academic institutions have almost become public undertakings. This explains why the number of elite institutions is fast receding.

II.
AN ADMINISTRATOR

The Principal is the chief-executive officer of an academic institution. As an administrator, he has to execute the policies laid down by the Board of Managements and do everything possible to improve efficiency. In this capacity, the Principal should be a good

1. *Leader,* not because of his post but because of his qualities of head and heart
2. *Motivator* of students and staff
3. *Efficient* administrator.

It will be advisable to have brief narration of these three.

1. **Principal : A Leader**

Normally a leader is one who exercises an out standing influence on the activities of the group-members and also gets influenced by the opinion of the followers. "The leader is said to give the lead, make acceptable suggestions, show the way, act as a model for others, advance opinions or give commands, which are respected and carried."

A person may be called a formal leader because of his official position. A Principal is a leader because of his official position. But to become a real leader, a Principal should try to acquire the qualities of a leader. There are more than eighty qualities out of which the main ones are —

i) *Physically fit and hardworking* —A sick person cannot be an effective leader. He must be able to work hard.
ii) *Intellectually fit* — A leader must be an intelligent person. He must have a quick grasp of things.
iii) *Academically sound with vast general knowledge* — A leader of an academic institution must be known as a well read person and having good knowledge of his subject.
iv) *Morally sensitive* — He must be honest, just, truthful idealist, kind, etc.
v) *Sweet tongued and well mannered.*
vi) *Tactful.*
vii) *Good Communicator.*
viii) *Self-restrained.*
ix) *Imaginative.*
x) *Having high sense of responsibility.*
xi) *Pushing, dynamic and determined.*
xii) *Imperturable* — Balanced, optimist, strong willed, patient, forbearing.
xii) *Courageous*

All of these qualities can be acquired by constant efforts. They are not necessarily to be inborn. Self-analysis and introspection is necessary to develop them.

2. An Excellent Motivator

Psychologists further opine that motivation depends upon needs. These needs can be biological — hunger, thirst, sex, etc., and psychological such as security, love, social approval, belonging, etc. Prescott has classified them in three categories and Edward in fifteen.

The prime duty of a successful Principal is to motivate students, teachers and non-teachers. He should inspire them. He should develop in them a feeling of belonging to the institution. They should be inspired to take a pride in being associated with the institution. This sense of belonging and pride will go a long way in motivating the students and teachers.

Reward and punishment are twin techniques to motivate students, non-teachers and teachers. Out of the two, punishment must be used sparingly. It is the reward which generates interest. This reward may by in the form of praise, approval, cash, or kind.

Sometimes, actual participation in activities generates the feeling of belonging to the institution. This is the key to motivation.

Sharing responsibility with others also inspires them and motivates them.

So, a Principal should set high goals, repeatedly remind students, teachers and non-teachers about them, create a need for such an elite institution, decentralise power, develop a sense of belonging to and pride for the institution, use the technique of reward and punishment and set an example by his own actions. All this and much more will motivate students, teachers and non-teachers and help in the achievement of the goal and their sustenance.

3. Efficient Administrator

A Principal should be a very efficient administrator. He must make meticulous arrangements for every activity, great or small, before time. For example, the lists of admitted students, class attendance registers, dusters, chalk-sticks, opening and cleaning of class rooms and furniture, etc., must be ready before the start of lectures in the college so that teachers and students may not have to waste their time in waiting.

Principal, as a *Manger has to take decisions in one* of the following ways :

A. *Autocratic* :
a) Taking decisions on his own, on the basis of information with him,
b) Taking decisions after gathering information from some individuals separately or in groups,
c) Discarding others' opinions as presumptuous interference.

B. *Democratic* :
a) Discussing with concerned persons and arriving at a consensus for decision,
b) Speaking out his opinion but getting guided by the opinions expressed.

C. *Laissez faire* Complete absence of interference from the top. If the subordinates are highly competent, skilled and dependable, then this may give the best results.

No one way is absolutely good or bad. A Principal must use different methods at different times as the circumstances demand. Dr. S.C. Gupta, Ex Director of Higher Education, U.P. said, "I as a Principal at Gyanpur used to prepare the resolution which was to be passed by the Faculty before the meeting to avoid wasteful discussion. This resolution worked as a basis for discussions. In cultural matters, I found that the students did nothing. They just hired singers, dancers, etc. — all film or Radio artists. In this case I became an autocrat and said that no outsider will be hired; students themselves will have to prepare. I did not get the cooperation of Faculty but I was able to enthuse students by my direct interaction with them and I succeeded in implementation of my decisions". So, a Principal must be Democratic at one time and Autocratic at another.

The decisions can be of two types — those which are very important and those that are not so important. The "garden — variety decisions" like what brand of cycle or pencil to purchase should be made instantaneously. Therc is no point in deferring for three weeks a decision that can be taken in three seconds and corrected inexpensively later, if found wrong. The other type — important ones should also be made quickly, as far as possible, but only after due deliberations. Let us remember, delay can lead to serious consequences.

In matters of decisions President Roosevelt had a small plate on his table on which it was inscribed, "Buck stops here", i.e., neither decisions will be delayed nor will the matter be transferred to some subordinate to take decision.

In this regard, the Principal should think and decide which mattes should come to him for decision and which should be decided at a lower level. I know of a Vice-Chancellor, who in his enthusiasm, started getting all files to his desk and started taking decisions. So, he became a Registrar, a Deputy Registrar, a Finance officer and a Vice- Chancellor — all rolled into one. Obviously, his subordinates had a permanent holiday and he had no respite. He could not devote time to serious and important matters. Administratively, he was a failure. So the Principal should delegate authority to responsible and well-meaning persons in as many matters as possible. He must just keep a watch on the delegated matters.

As an administrators, a Principal has to face various problems. For this, be must —

i) Diagnose the problem properly,
ii) Arrive at an optimum solution,
iii) Implement it, and
iv) Check that it worked. If it failed, again start the same process.

To elaborate this point an illustration of a tap was given by an expert.

A tap was leaking. This appeared to be a problem. But this was not the problem. This was the result of a problem. Just as students agitation is not a problem; it is a result of one or more than one problem.

Why was the tap leaking? Its washer could be defective, its ferrule could be defective, etc. So, check up every item and find out the real cause of the problem. In case of students' agitation, know what the causes are. Are they not getting the drinking water; are the rooms not properly dusted off; or what is their prime demand. The Principal should get all facts.

How can the leaking tap be repaired—by changing the washer, or changing the ferrule or changing the whole tap? Do what will give the optimum results — the best result at the lowest cost in the shortest possible time. In case of students' agitation, once the cause has been identified, remove it and have a direct dialogue with the students. It so happened at Almora that students went on agitation. They wanted several new subjects to be started. The Principal had a direct interaction with them. He suggested that for the first time we should concentrate only on two new subjects. They agreed. But how to get it done. He suggested that without political pressure no result will come. So, the Principal suggested that we must contact Mr. Pant, the Chief Minister. The trick worked.

In the case of a malfunctioning tap, once it has been repaired, check it. If it works properly it is allright. Otherwise again start the same process. This applies equally to the problems cropping up before the Principal in a college.

In the light of the above discussion, the Principal should ponder over the following.

1. *Objectives*

A Principal is a Leader. One of the important functions of a leader is to make organization know the objectives and concentrate on them. It is not easy to concentrate. But repeated reminders and by setting personal examples, results do come. So, make the objectives clear.

2. *Delegation of Authority*

Delegate authxority in as many matters as one possibly can because that creates a climate in which people grow and one cannot do all things by oneself. And while delegating matters do as much supervision work as possible yourself and delegate maximum important matters to others.

Give full liberty after authority has been delegated. Keep a watchful eye. If things seem going amiss at sometimes, give advice and set them on the right track.

3. *Own Subordinates Mistakes*

Just like you, your subordinates can also commit mistakes — pull them up privately and humanely but protect them outwardly. Own their mistakes as yours as they act on your behalf. You will thereby command their loyalty.

4. *Proper Selection, Training and Placement*

A person once appointed cannot be easily chucked off. So do not easily listen to recommendations in matters of appointments. You are engaged in the sacred duty of making the lives of young boys and girls. Even a second rater will be a hazard. So, just go for the very best.

Train up the selected man conscientiously, carefully and properly.

Place a person where he can prove the best. Keep a watch and evaluate him. Tell him his mistakes in an affectionate and elderly way.

5. *Punishment*

Punishment to an employee is unpleasant; it should however be done if things turn so serious that it cannot be avoided. But do it after giving the person concerned repeated opportunities to improve and after making a fool proof case on the records as none takes the punishment easily and seeks protection from all possible agencies, executive as well as legal.

6. *Reorganise*

Reorganisation should be gone through as a major surgery, well planned and swiftly executed. It will train up new aspirants and the possibilities of generation of self-interest will be minimised.

7. *Do Work Studies*

You must try to evaluate how much work can be done in a day at each table. Check up if the output is according to this work study. If not, pull the workers. Do this checking regularly.

8. *Know Your Men and Help them : Love begets Love*

You must know your associates — teaches, non-teachers and students — not only by name but as much details about them as you can. You must know their personal problems, their past, their future aspirations, their capacities, the atmosphere of their families. Treat yourself as their elder and well-wisher. Plunge in their personal problems and help them as much as you can. You will command their respect and loyalty which in turn will help the institution. The motto should be: *'Be first at crucial moments.'*

9. *Promises*

Be wary of giving promises but once given, keep them up. The world is divided into two classes of people : the few who make good of their promises and the many who do not. Get in column A and stay there. You will be valuable, wherever you are.

10. *Listing to Complaints and Suggestions*

To listen to complaints and suggestions is two-way rewarding. People with complaints want some one to listen, and the closer is the attention of the higher up who handles the complaint, the quicker their ire goes out. Moreover, it gives you an opportunity to know facts and, if need be, to remedy them.

Keep boxes at different places for students to put in their suggestions. Meet small groups of a cross section of students, teachers and non-teachers to hear their complaints and suggestions.

11. *Apologise*

"To err is human" and you can't claim to be above this universal truth. So, admit your mistakes openly and without reservation and encourage your association also to do likewise. Never castigate. Babies fall down again and again before they learn to walk. If you scold or beat a baby every time he falls, he will never care much for walking.

While apologising, look in the eyes of the person and not to the ground.

Be plain in apologising. Never pretend to be doing anything else. Never dilute an apology by making excuses. Do not deprive the other person of a chance to be forgiving. Since most people enjoy being magnanimous, the unreserved and plain apology leaves both parties feeling better about themselves.

12. *Be Well Informed and up to date in every Matter that you Handle*

Do not take things casually. Be thorough that is the road to success.

13. *Do not Talk Loosely or Lightly : Be Matter of Fact but be Sweet and Reasonable*

When you talk loosely, people start taking liberties.

14. *Meet People with Smiles*

It makes people at ease. They go back with a good feeling.

15. *Do Not Deviate From Truth*

Lie has no ground to stand. It is exposed sooner than you think, it will be. Then your whole credibility will be lost and people will hesitate in taking you at your word.

16. *Publicly Praise Good Work*

Praise inspires others. It generates a competitive spirit also.

17. *Always be Ready to Enter into Dialogue*

Despotism breeds revolt. Talking matters with students, teachers or non-teachers, diffuses the tension of a situation and leads to an amicable solution. But never compromise on principles or morality. Initially, it may appear to be troublesome, but people start understanding and appreciating you sooner than you think they will.

18. *Be Bold, Firm and Calm*

Sometimes in the process of being heard, you will have to face ugly situations. But for that fear, do not delay the process. Delay will aggravate them. So, handle them boldly, calmly and firmly without any loss of time.

19. *Plan in Details*

Every change, every activity and every function should be planned on paper to the minutest details. Responsible persons must be made in-charges for various things. You must keep yourself free to meet emergencies and supervise matters.

20. *Execute the Plans Smoothly*

21. *Be on the Lookout for Welfare Schemes*

22. *Never Compromise with Evil*

23. *Be Strict in Admission and Go by Merit*

Meritorious students will be less trouble-some. It will be easier to chisel them and make them better men.

If you are forced to take sub-standard students, fix a minimum percentage of such admission and give it the form of a rule.

24. *Thanks*

Do not be miser in giving this neglected form of compensation. It may do wonders.

25. *Develop a Sense of Belonging and a Passion to Work*

Do not think that you are in service. Think that this institution is yours. Only then you will develop a passion to work for its all round integrated development. This feeling of belonging should also be inculcated in the students, non-teachers and teachers. Once, it comes, a climate is created and thereafter people learn by atmosphere and tradition. In Japan this sense of belonging is the key to all progress.

26. *Stick on Neatness and Cleanliness*

An institution is know by its appearance. Keep the walls, bathrooms, roads, *etc.*, neat and clean. Sweeping, dusting of class rooms and bathrooms must be a daily affair. Teachers, students and non-teachers should also be educated to do nothing to retard the cleanliness of the building or the campus.

27. *Develop Work-Culture*

When a person enters a job, he has a desire to work. But the atmosphere, the work-culture of the place soon makes him indifferent. The Principal must closely watch this work-culture of his institution and try to improve it. Here are a few tips. A good Principal should try to find more of such tips and execute them.

a) If a good performance is observed and the worker — teacher, non-teacher and student is patted, he gets due encouragement. A feeling develops that he is being watched. For example, if an article of a teacher is published in a foreign journal or he takes regular and even extra-classes to finish his courses, and he is praised for this good work done by him, he gets motivated. Similarly, if a good player, a good debator, a good N.C.C. cadet is praised for his good work and for bringing honour to the institution it creates a healthy atmosphere. It has been noted that today real merit or real good effort is not recognised but pseudo-merit or pseudo good effort is recognised. This will be not only unproductive but give wrong signals. This should never be done.

b) If a person does good work constantly and he is publicly rewarded, he gets extremely motivated. But this reward in terms of money will have not much importance. It must be in the form of an artistic article and a certificate preceded by full throated public ovation. This sort of recognition is beyond any calculable monetary value.

c) If a bad work is not connived at and no reprimand is inflicted immediately, it is likely that the person concerned—a teacher, a non-teacher or a student — will become more negligent in work. He will develop a sense of immunity and take negligence as his privilege. On the contrary, a knowledge that he is being observed will make him alert and active.

d) If a person puts his best efforts but he is unfortunate in not getting desired output, even then his work must be noticed and he must be praised for his efforts. The feeling that the effort and not the result, is of greater importance is pace-setter.

e) It is desirable to keep office *marginally* short of men, space and resources. It helps in making people show their best to meet this shortage and give the optimal results.

f) The office must be divided into sections. Each section should be small and compact. It must be put under an in-charge. The present times are of specialists and not of generalists. This will give a feeling to the workers that they are specialists and not generalists. This will also help in fixing responsibility and making people accountable. In such a case the incharge, with his team, will try to put his very best.

g) Every person has his strength and weaknesses. The Principal should know the good and bad points of each worker. He should place a person in such a way that his good point or strength is put to the best use and his weaknesses remain curbed. The Principal should also try to help the individual in overcoming the weaknesses. In such a situation, placement of worker acquires importance.

h) Every person has his aptitude. If a work is given as per aptitude, the worker remains satisfied and the output is optimum. Normally people can be classified under three categories:

i) *Yoges* — They are mentally alert, have new ideas, new theories and are good innovators.
ii) *Commissars* — They are down to earth, good organisers with a capacity to get the work done.
iii) *In Between* — Bulk of the people fall between these two extremes.

It is desirable to know the category of an individual and place him at the right place. Wrong placement may be troublesome.

1. Aptitude, placement and training are important in developing a good work culture. The following points are worth thinking and acting upon though they may appear to be contradictory to each other:

   i) To know ones aptitude, one is to be tried at various jobs and thereafter fixed at the right place.
   ii) A feeling that one is monopolist of a particular job is not good. It inflates ego and makes one arrogant. So, at least two more persons having the same aptitude be trained up to do the job, and only the best be selected. The feeling that others can take up the job if he is negligent or careless, will keep the worker trim.
   iii) Every worker needs to be exposed to the latest techniques of work concerning him. He needs training. So, it will always be better if the Principal is on a lookout for such short courses and depute his people. In the long run this practice will prove productive.

j) Today , the Western style of functioning imposed on Indian workers seems to be out-dated. It was profit motive-oriented and so autocratic. It created disintegration, groupism and hostilities, generating a sense of class superiority and inferiority. The Japanese method of work culture seems to be the latest — the incoming work culture. It is very much akin to the Hindu Joint Family system in which the Head of the Family, *Karta* gave a patient hearing to every family member but once he decided his course of action every one followed it wholeheartedly. This was because every one has a feeling that the *Karta* is his well wisher and that of the family. He has a sense of belonging and pride in the family. The Japanese have tried to create a Family work culture. They have taken the following steps:

i) The recruitment is done at the lowest ladder and all higher posts are filled in by promotions. This may be adopted, as far as rules and situations permit.
ii) The President, or the Chairman tries to tell one and all the goal of the concern — Long-term goal and yearly goal. To achieve his overall yearly goal, sectional sub-goals are determined and workers of the concerned sections are told their goals. This is repeated off an on.
iii) Weekly or daily general meetings are held in which the Chief-Executive tells the workers what is to be done, what are the problems and invites suggestions. He never dictates his opinion and decision. Every worker feels he is a part of the set-up and knows things.
iv) Sub-section incharges also hold morning meetings daily and tell what work is to be done, sorts out the individual problem and encourages people that in the national interest, and in the interest of the concern, this is to be achieved. Patriotism and sense of belonging to the concern is preached. The results are excellent.
v) The Chief-Executive and sectional incharges, tactfully sell the idea what should be done to achieve the goal. A sort of debate starts. Normally, the workers agree with the suggestion. It is then taken to be the workers decision. Every worker feels that it is he who has taken the decision and so it is his duty to execute it successfully.
vi) The British policy of transferring people after an interval

of time is not good. Transfers presuppose that one is a generalist and not a specialist. Moreover, they hamper the development of sense of belonging. In todays competitive world, generalists have no place, So, transfers should be as minimum as possible.

When transfers are minimum, promotions should be result-oriented.

If the worker is mediocre, he should not be promoted out of turn. But if a worker has initiative, he may be considered for out-of-turn promotion but his supremacy over even his seniors should be a well established and well accepted fact.

If the worker is a conformist, he should not be considered for out of turn promotions. But if the worker is innovative, he should be given out of turn promotions.

Seniority should not be the only criterion for out of turn promotions. Results, innovation, dynamism, etc. should be the basis for such promotions.

If a Joint Hindu Family Culture of mutual love, respect, sense of belonging and pride can be inculcated among the individuals connected with the institution, it will have a way smooth enough for becoming an elite institution producing integrated, balanced and developed end-products, who will have a ready market.

INDEX